A POCKET FULL OF SHELLS

Book 1: An Irish Family Saga

by

Jean Reinhardt

D1143910

This book is dedicated to my parents
Jack and Kitty

AUTHOR BIO

Jean Reinhardt was born in Louth, grew up in Dublin and lived in Alicante, Spain for almost eight years. With five children and four grandchildren, life is never dull. She now lives in Ireland and loves to read, write, listen to music and spend time with family and friends. When Jean isn't writing she likes to take long walks through the woods and on the beach.

Jean writes poetry, short stories and novels. Her favourite genres are Young Adult and Historical Fiction.

https://jeanreinhardt.wordpress.com/

https://www.facebook.com/JeanReinhardt Writer

https://twitter.com/jeanreinhardt1

Other books by the author:
The Finding Trilogy: a young adult suspense series.
Book 1: Finding Kaden
Book 2: Finding Megan
Book 3: Finding Henry Brubaker
Can all be found on Amazon, Createspace and Smashwords.

ACKNOWLEDGEMENTS

I would like to thank the following people for their much appreciated support and encouragement:

Sharon for giving me a boost when I felt like giving up.

Eileen and Carol for reading the story as it was being written and encouraging me so much.

Joan for proofing the final edit and finding all the stuff I missed.

Pascaline for such a lovely and enthusiastic reaction to the finished story.

You, the reader, who has taken the time to sample my work and show an interest in it.

Last, but not least, my mother, who read every chapter as it was written and made it all worthwhile.

A Note from the Author

This is a story I have loosely based around my great, great grandmother's parents. Her name was Catherine McGrother and she was born in 1846 to James McGrother and Mary (Roarke) McGrother. They went on to have at least four more children after Catherine, who was born at a time when Ireland was in the grip of what came to be known as An Gorta Mór (The Great Hunger). Catherine lived to be one hundred and two years of age, my mother was twelve when she died and remembers her well. I have been able to get a glimpse of this remarkable woman through the eyes of my mother, who is also called Catherine.

How did James, a fisherman, and Mary manage to raise a family at a time when one person in every nine inhabitants died between the years 1845 and 1852? From the records I have discovered that their last child was born in Ireland in 1862, so it seems they were not among the one and a half million who emigrated in the hopes of a better life elsewhere. Many of those hopeful, starving people died on the 'coffin' ships sailing to their new destination, or shortly after they arrived. The population of Ireland is just over four and a half million today, but it is estimated that upwards of seventy million people throughout the world claim Irish descent.

Most of the story in this book is fictitious, with historical facts setting the scene in Dundalk, Liverpool and Sunderland, places that have a connection to my mother's family. I wanted to show the reader how people coped in their own way with the difficult situations they found themselves in. I created a relationship between James and Mary that turned their lives into a love story – it may have been the case, I like to think so anyway.

Jean Reinhardt 2013

CHAPTER ONE

Since they were children James McGrother had loved Mary Roarke, but never let on in case his brothers found out. They would have given him a hard time over it. Instead, he tried to ignore her, calling her names when any of his family were nearby. They would chastise him for his treatment of her, saying *"Leave poor Mary alone,"* and, *"What did the little mite do to deserve that?"* It wasn't until they were in their mid-teens that James purposefully tried to get her attention, which she then chose to ignore. When Mary eventually paid heed to him it was purely the result of an accident.

Searching for bilberries on Fraughan Sunday, a tradition in Ireland on the last Sunday in July, named after the fruit, Mary tripped and slid down a bank of grass. In his hurry to help her, James caught his foot on the exposed root of a tree and toppled head first down the green slope, passing her by in the process. He came to a stop at the bottom of the incline and lay flat on his back, eyes closed. A few seconds later Mary landed beside him and took hold of his hand, calling his name. Fearing the worst, she put her face close to his, hoping to feel the breath coming from his nostrils. When he sensed the nearness of her, James opened his eyes and kissed her cheek, then closing them again, he flinched – waiting for the slap that was surely coming. Instead, he was aware of the softest brush of her lips against his skin.

They were married the following year, in 1845, as soon as Mary turned seventeen, James being eighteen. That was the first year of the potato blight. Everyone coped as best they could, believing that the following year would be better, but the winter was harsh and there was no money for rent or food. To make matters worse, Mary was pregnant and her father was missing. James had been living with his wife's family when the fever struck her mother. The couple moved in with one of his married sisters, at the insistence of Mary's mother. The only reason she obeyed her and remained outside her parents' cabin on her visits, was because of their unborn child. It broke her heart not to be able to do more for her sick mother and she cried herself to sleep every night in James's arms.

The neighbours, Mary's relatives, who only had one child, took in the three younger children. Not long after their mother's death, their foster parents decided to take up an offer from the landlord of a ship's passage to America. James and Mary knew it would be impossible for them to care for her younger brother and two sisters and made the heart-breaking decision to let them go with the others. She had lost her father, mother and her siblings in the space of six months. James thought he would lose her too, and his unborn child, because of the grief she was suffering.

When Mary was eight months pregnant, James's brothers also took up the offer of transport to another country. They had relatives in county Durham in the north east of England and there was work to be had on the docks and in the foundries. They begged him and Mary to go with them. Even his married sisters and their husbands and children were leaving. None of them had the money to pay the rent and knew they would soon be facing evictions. James thought long and hard about what he should do. His young wife was so weak from grief and hunger, he was afraid the journey on an overcrowded vessel would kill her, or their child – or both.

At first his brothers were angry and upset at his refusal to join them. His sisters were more understanding, if any of them had been pregnant they would not have risked the journey either. James promised that as soon as Mary and the baby were fit to travel, they would join the rest of the family in England but in his heart he knew he would never go.

The entire family had agreed to leave their homes on the same day and make their way to Dundalk where they would board the ferry to Liverpool. Mary could not keep up the pace and James told his family to go on ahead, for fear they would miss the boat, as the landlord had already arranged their passage. The twenty mile journey would have been fine for a well-nourished pregnant woman. But they hadn't eaten since the day before, and it wasn't much of a meal at that. James watched as the last of his family disappeared around a bend in the road.

"I'm so sorry," said Mary wiping her eyes, "I really tried to keep up with everyone."

The young man kissed his wife's forehead and lifted her up in his arms, carrying her until his strength gave out. Looking behind a hedgerow, James saw a hollow in the ground and made a gap so that Mary could get through the tangled branches. He managed to make a scalp which was even worse than a scalpeen. It was no more than a hole in the ground with a few rocks and sods of grass to give some bit of shelter for the night. During those hard years of hunger and evictions in Ireland, homeless families made scalpeens out of tumble-down cottages and lived in them as best they could. Luckily for the young couple it didn't rain that night.

James knew that his brothers would be calling on their aunt and uncle in the village of Blackrock, on the way to Dundalk. They would say their farewells and let them know he would be arriving with Mary. His aunt would be worried if he didn't get there the next day, so as soon as it was light they set off. He was excited about showing his young wife the ocean, she had never seen it before. As the morning passed, the grey sky filled with angry clouds and the young couple knew a storm was gathering. Again, James carried Mary, until his legs buckled under him and she jumped from his arms just before his knees hit the hard ground.

The worried look on his wife's face made him laugh." Are you afraid it might be your turn to carry me?" teased James.

"This is as good a place as any to take a rest," Mary said as she sat down beside him.

A strange noise came from behind a nearby bush and James got up to investigate. He shouted for Mary to run, as he grabbed a thick branch and broke it off in one swift movement. She didn't have to be told twice, as she could hear the snarling and snapping of angry dogs. James caught up with her and helped her along, all the while looking back in case they were being chased by the starving animals.

Mary came to an abrupt halt, a stitch in her side." I can't ... take ... another ... step," she was out of breath.

The road behind them was quiet with no sign of the dogs, so James suggested they sit for a while to regain their strength.

"How many were there?" asked Mary, breathing easier.

"Only two," James said. "They were fighting over something. One of them saw me, but he was having a tug of war with the other dog over an old bone. They won't bother us, you can relax now."

12

The weary couple had been sitting a while, lost in their own thoughts, when all of a sudden, something leapt up behind them and landed on Mary's back. Before the scream could leave her lips, James was standing, stick in hand, shouting at the top of his voice. He made a ferocious swipe at the animal with all the strength he could muster, sending it flying and yelping into the air. Two more dogs came at them from behind the low hedgerow. The young man stood between them and his wife, snarling back at them, threatening with the stick. Another two arrived, one with a bone in his mouth, but kept their distance.

"Stand up, Mary. Make yourself bigger than them. Be aggressive, shout and snarl. It will frighten them off."

The adrenaline pumping through her spurred the young woman into action, and she outdid her husband in growling at the pack. The dogs, whimpering, turned tail and ran, leaving James and Mary coughing and laughing.

"I hope I never find myself on the receiving end of your anger," laughed James. "Those animals will still be running tomorrow, they got such a fright. I almost went with them."

Mary went very quiet. When she did speak it was in a hushed tone. "Tell me the truth, was that a human thigh bone in the dog's mouth?"

"Yes, it was. But it's an old bone, maybe from a grave," replied James.

Mary sat down and cried huge sobs that sent shudders through her body. Her young husband sat beside her, rubbing her back, trying to soothe her.

"Calm down, love. Take deep breaths, think of the baby. It's the shock that has you so upset."

"No, it's not that at all. The thought struck me that my father could have died in a hedgerow with a pack of dogs fighting over his bones. Nobody has heard any news. How will I ever know what happened to him, James?"

All of the grief she had stored in her heart seemed to be spreading convulsively through her thin, swollen body. James had never seen his wife this upset, not even when her mother died and her younger brother and sisters left to go to America.

Nothing he could say would make any difference to how Mary felt, so they sat there, on the side of the road, until the sobs got softer. James had one arm around his wife and the other was still holding the stick, in case the dogs returned.

After a long time, Mary sighed deeply, stood up and brushed down her dusty clothes.

"Right, James, we should get a move on, before the storm sets in. I've done my grieving. You and this baby are what's important to me now."

Mary held her hand out to her husband, who was still sitting on the ground.

She helped him up and said, "By the way, next time you see a pack of dogs don't lie to me, pretending there's only two. I wouldn't have got such a fright if I had known what to expect," and she slapped him lightly on the back of the head as they set out on the last leg of their journey.

CHAPTER TWO

Hand in hand, the exhausted couple stood waiting for the weather-beaten door to open. The noise of the sea behind her was a strange and frightening sound to the young woman. James turned to watch the waves crashing on the shore.

"Look at the sea, Mary. Don't be afraid, it's too far away to harm us."

As he was speaking the door creaked open and a pair of gnarled hands grabbed hold of the young woman's shoulders.

"Oh you poor wee thing, come in out of the weather. What a day to be travelling, and in your condition too," James's aunt Annie had been waiting for their arrival all morning.

A large, black cauldron of soup made from fish heads and kelp was bubbling over the fire. Nothing had ever tasted so good to the young visitors. They hadn't eaten for two days and the walk had left them on the verge of collapse. Annie watched as her guests tried not to wolf down the warm liquid, but hunger overtook them and in no time the soup was gone. Mary turned the empty wooden bowl around in her hand, examining it closely.

"I'm afraid there's no more in the pot, my love. Pat has gone hunting and won't be back for a while, he might be lucky this time," said Annie. "You should lie down for a bit and get some sleep. We can have salted herring for supper. My Pat is a fine fisherman and I can't remember the last time we had no fish in this house, fresh or salted."

Embarrassed, Mary apologized, "I'm sorry, I didn't mean to be rude. I was admiring this bowl. It's beautiful, so smooth."

Picking one of the bowls up from the table, Annie ran her rough old fingers around its shiny base.

"I have six of them, left to me by my mother. It was her older brother who made them for a wedding present. I think I will pass them on to you when my time is up. You are the first person to look on them as lovingly as I do."

"Don't talk of such things, Aunt Annie," said James. "There's years left in you yet."

"Ahh, of course there is. Well now, let's get this young wife of yours to bed. She's exhausted, poor wee mite."

Annie stood up from the table and led the way to a stairway that curled behind a chimney. It reached up to a small windowless loft room, heated by the fire below. A bed of straw-filled sacks was waiting to be slept on, and Mary lay herself down as gently as she could, not wanting to disturb her unborn child.

Downstairs James and Annie spoke in hushed voices.

"Why did you not go with your brothers and sisters to England? There's nothing for you here except hunger," Annie whispered.

"How could I bring Mary when she is heavily pregnant? There's talk of the fever there too. She would surely catch it," said James. "Besides, you always told me I was your favourite, and we need grandparents for our child."

He took his aunt's crooked hand in his and gave her the smile that always melted her heart, even when he deserved a scolding.

"You can take that grin off your face, it doesn't work anymore," Annie said unconvincingly. "I never minded too much about us not having any children of our own – you made up for that in lots of ways. Pat took great pleasure in teaching you to fish and hunt, especially as you were orphaned so young. Your visits here gave us the joy of being parents for a while. We will always be grateful for that, my boy."

"My brothers were thankful to have somewhere to send me, I was such a handful."

A loud, creaking sound made them turn their faces from the fire. James jumped up from his seat and ran towards the rain sodden shape that came through the door.

"Wait till I get these wet clothes off my back, son, or we will both be soaked," Pat said.

He shut out the storm and hung a dripping cape on a hook near the fire. That done, the two men embraced warmly then stood apart, examining each other closely.

"You look even younger, Uncle Pat, if that's possible for the ugly old crow that you are," James said, ducking as the older man playfully made a swipe at him.

"Quick as ever now, aren't you, my boy." Pat loved the way they could just pick up from where they had left off two years before.

"You're not too old to have a spanking, you know, and I'm not too soft to give it to you," said Pat, still trying to catch his young opponent.

James stood up straight and squared his shoulders. "I'm a married man of nineteen now, and soon to be a father."

The young man flexed his arms to show off his biceps and Pat stepped back to look him up and down, acknowledging that James had certainly become a man.

"With no land to work this past year how did you manage to build muscle like that?" he asked.

James went quiet and sat down on the bench beside Annie.

"Breaking stones for a penny a day. I was one of the lucky ones. I had enough strength to have a heap of them by evening. Some men were too old or too sick and got nothing. Now and again I gave my pile of stones away, but not very often, I'm ashamed to say. It's really bad in Monaghan, the whole county is starving. People are either leaving or dying." James held back bitter tears of frustration and anger.

"Now, now, son. Don't dwell on things you can do nothing about. Where is this young wife of yours, didn't you bring her with you, or is married life not what you expected? Have you run away already?" Pat teased, peering into the empty cauldron by the fire.

Annie stood beside him and looked into the pot. "Do you think we could get another broth out of those old fish heads, or are you going to surprise us with a nice rabbit?" she asked, not getting her hopes up.

"Sorry, love, I couldn't catch a thing. All the animals are hiding from the weather. I'm sure I heard a rabbit laughing at me for being out on such a bad day as this," Pat joked.

"Never mind, tomorrow is another day, we can collect seaweed and cockles and we still have some salted herring left," said Annie. "Sit down there by the fire and let James tell us about his lovely wife."

The young man's face clouded over as he told his aunt and uncle about the fate of Mary's family. Her father, Michael Roarke, a stone mason, had gone to search for work in Leitrim, having heard they were looking for men there to build a bridge.

"I almost went with him, but Mary begged me not to go," said James. "If she had not been pregnant I would have left with her father. We were living in her parent's house and I knew she would be taken care of, but I stayed to keep her from fretting. A month went by and there was no word from him. Then Mary's mother got the fever and sent us all away. Her three younger children went to stay with a neighbour and one of my sister's took us in. Going twice a day to leave some broth or meal and fresh water in the doorway, Mary was not allowed to step inside for fear of catching the sickness herself. Even I was forbidden to enter the house. Screaming and shouting at us to keep our distance, the poor woman used a long stick to push her empty bowls towards the door. When we filled them she insisted we return the food to her in the same manner."

"Oh, the poor unfortunate woman," exclaimed Annie.

"Each day, Mary's mother would tell us she was on the mend and feeling better," James continued. "We were beginning to believe it might be true and I could see the relief in Mary's face after every visit. One evening as we walked towards the cottage we could see it had no roof. The neighbouring homes were empty and derelict. The Roarkes' cabin was the last one on that side of the village to keep its roof. Panicking, thinking it had collapsed on top of her mother, we ran to the door and pulled away the sticks and thatch that lay in a heap on the floor – but the poor woman wasn't there. On our way to

21

the village we had passed a group of men pushing a cart, so we turned back and caught up with them. We knew they had been collecting the bodies of a family who had died in a neighbouring village. They had also been pulling in the roofs of empty homes to discourage squatters. Mary begged them to pull back the sheet covering the mound of twisted forms. As long as I live, I will never forget the despair in Mary's cry as the cold, blue eyes of her dead mother stared up at us," James looked into the fire's dying flames. "That was the day I became a man, Uncle Pat."

Later that evening, when Mary had joined them, there was salted herring for supper with a little Indian meal, a type of corn shipped in from America. It helped to take the edge off their hunger. Pat had built up the fire to cook the cornmeal that Annie had mixed with water and formed into small flat cakes. These she placed around the base and sides of the empty cauldron to brown. The four of them ate in silence, the storm howling around the cottage and the wind whistling through the gaps in the door.

There was a settle bed each side of the fireplace and Annie got Mary to lie down on one of them. She could see the young woman was still very tired.

"If you are more comfortable there, then you and James can stay down here for the night. It's all the same to us, upstairs is just as warm."

Their cottage was one of the few to have a chimney and a loft.

"Thank you, Annie, I would rather stay here tonight, I'm so exhausted. I don't fancy climbing the stairs again. Are you sure you don't mind?" asked Mary.

"Not at all, in fact I'm not so lively myself this evening so I'm off to bed as soon as I bank the fire. Pat, go on up there and warm the straw for me," said Annie, winking at Mary.

Before heading for the stairs she kissed the young couple on their foreheads and wished them a good night's sleep.

When they were alone, James lay beside Mary and placed his hand over her swollen belly. As soon as the baby felt the weight it jumped.

"That's a fine kick he has. There's nothing to worry about with this little one." James was trying to allay his wife's fears about her lack of food throughout her pregnancy.

"How do you know it's a boy? What will you do if we have a girl? Won't you love her just the same?" Mary asked.

James kissed the back of her neck. "I will love her as much as I do her mother," he whispered.

"No, you won't," said Mary. "You must love this child more than me. Do you hear?"

"Don't fret so. I will, if that's what makes you happy," but James knew in his heart it wasn't true.

CHAPTER THREE

As the weeks went by and the days got brighter, James and Pat had plenty of opportunity to fish and hunt. Mary tried to help Annie in the small garden attached to the cottage, but she tired easily. The sea no longer frightened her, except whenever the men were out in the boats fishing. On those occasions she would stand by the small window looking out to sea, praying for their safe return. Annie told her she would get used to it, in time. The women collected cockles and seaweed. Each day James could see his wife getting stronger, the pale, grey tinge to her skin being replaced by a healthy glow.

Mary loved to walk along the shore. The sound of the waves made a deep impression on her, whether it was the pounding crash of an angry sea or the gentle kiss of water as it lapped around bare feet on firm sand. Annie was constantly chastising her for paddling in cold water, saying it would give her a chill, or harm the baby. Mary would listen to the well-meant advice, nodding her head in agreement. However, each time she returned to the beach the pull of the sea was irresistible and more often than not, her feet would stay rooted to the sand waiting for the water to roll over them. Many a time James and Pat saw Mary splashing about, but never said a word to Annie.

It was on a cold, sunny spring day, while the men were repairing nets and laying them over the rocks, that James saw his wife collapse into the water. He shouted to Pat and they both ran to help her up.

"I got such a terrible pain, I couldn't stay upright," she said. "I think the baby is coming. Bring me back to Annie, quickly."

Carrying her to the cottage James called out his aunt's name repeatedly. Annie was tending the small vegetable patch behind the house and heard him before he was even in the gate. They lay Mary down on the bed by the fire just as another wave of pain hit her.

"How many times has that happened, is it regular?" asked Annie, stoking up the fire.

"I have been having a few small pains all morning but nothing like this. I thought it was the baby moving about," Mary gasped as another band of pain tightened around her abdomen.

"Pat, go fetch Kitty Carroll and be quick about it. James get more water on the boil." Annie was panicking inside but outwardly she appeared calm and composed.

Mary cried out with each painful contraction and James held her hand while listening to his aunt's instructions. As he wiped the young woman's brow he assured her that Annie knew exactly what to do.

"You must have delivered half the village with Kitty Carroll, isn't that so?" James's eyes were pleading with Annie to agree with him, even though it wasn't true.

"Of course I did. Sure it's the poor mother who does all the work anyway. We just help her along. Keep a firm hold of your husband's hand, Mary, squeeze as tight as you can. It took both of you to get you this way – I don't see why James shouldn't feel any discomfort," said Annie.

She stood by the fire warming a soft blanket Mary had made for the birth of her child, praying silently for the appearance of Kitty Carroll.

Ten minutes later, which seemed more like an hour to everyone, a little head popped out into the world. Never was a husband more proud of his wife than James at that moment. There was a gust of wind as the door was swung open by the woman who really had delivered half of the village.

"Alright, son, you've done more than should be expected of you. Outside with you now and look after your uncle, he's wearing a hole in the path with his pacing up and down," said Kitty.

James kissed Mary and jumped up quickly, obeying Kitty's orders. On reaching the door he turned around for one last look and saw his daughter slip out of her mother's body. As he stepped outside, the baby let out a wail that could only have been produced by a fine pair of lungs.

"Only a female could make a sound like that," said Pat shaking his nephew's hand.

"How did you know? It *is* a girl, I saw her just before Kitty threw me out," said James, proudly.

"I was only jesting about the cry, but you have to agree, she's loud. She'll give us grief, I can tell, and we'll enjoy every minute of it," laughed Pat. "Come on, we're going to Paddy Mac's. We can wet the baby's head with a bit of his poitín. There'll be no more drink if the blight strikes again this year, you can't make poitín out of rotten skins."

Having checked with Annie and Kitty that everything was well with Mary and the baby, James asked the women if he should stay or go with his uncle. Mary told him she was exhausted and wanted to sleep and sent him off to boast about the fine daughter they had just produced. The two men walked towards the village, carrying some fish to trade for a well-deserved drink.

CHAPTER FOUR

Paddy Mac's cabin was warm and welcoming, packed tight with local men who had heard the news of a baby being born. He was Kitty Carroll's neighbour and whenever he saw her running off in a hurry, he knew there would be a baby's head to wet and would send one of his children to keep him informed on the progress. A big cheer rose from the crowded room as soon as Pat and James entered.

"How did ye all know so soon?" asked James looking around the sea of faces.

"That was the quickest labour I ever heard tell of, my poor young fella nearly ran the legs off himself spreading the news around the village before you got here," said Paddy Mac.

The door opened and more well-wishers poured into the crowded parlour.

James was touched by their kindness. Pat wasn't surprised by it. He knew the glimmer of hope a new life could bring to his neighbours at a time when many around them were sick, or dying, or leaving. There was a lot of friendly back slapping and congratulations going on while the men settled down to various low toned discussions about recent events. James, being a husband and a father, felt part of a unique circle. He now had a family to take care of and times were hard. There was strength in numbers, a well-known fact among fishermen, as a boat with a crew was better than one man on his own.

"The poor unfortunates at the workhouse are being fed Indian meal, as there's no potatoes," someone said.

"Last month, thirty six starving people from the town admitted themselves in just one day. Things are getting worse. One year of blight was bad enough, if we have another one we are all finished," said Paddy Mac.

A man standing next to Pat remarked, "That's not a place I would want to bring my family to. Only last week a twelve year old girl was brought before the magistrate and sentenced to a fortnight in Dundalk jail for absconding in workhouse clothes. Leaving the place isn't a crime, but taking the clothes with you is. Sure the poor mite didn't have a stitch to call her own."

Listening to what the men were saying, James silently swore he would never let that happen to his daughter. Between Mary and himself, with the help of his aunt and uncle, they would get through the hard times.

"Enough of this gloom and doom," said Pat. "My young nephew here and his good wife have brought a fine healthy child into our lives, with a pair of lungs that would shatter glass. No doubt she will keep the whole village awake over the next few months. I might be a more regular visitor from now on, Paddy Mac."

The whole place erupted with laughter. James was made drink another glass of the clear liquid, its tingling heat spreading through his body, right down to his toes.

Later that night, Pat and his young companion walked in silent contentment back to the cottage, through the still night air. James hiccupped as they entered, drawing a look of scorn from Annie.

"You two must be exhausted after all that celebrating. Go on up to bed, Pat, and don't make a sound. Mary and her little one are fast asleep. I'll be up as soon as I have finished here."

While Annie was speaking to his uncle, James sat on the floor close to the bed where his young wife and new-born daughter lay. He couldn't take his eyes off the baby, she looked so peaceful and content.

"Make the most of her quiet moments, there won't be too many of those for a while," Annie said, as if reading his thoughts. "James, son, come over here and sit by me, there's something I want to say to you."

The young man had to drag himself away from his daughter's side, shocked at the strong pull she already had on his heart.

"What is it, Aunt Annie? Did I do something wrong? I'm sorry about the drink, I'm not used to it," he said.

The old woman smiled and shook her head. "No, James, I'm not going to chastise you. I only want to give you a wee bit of advice. You can take it or leave it, I won't mind."

Annie pointed to the bed in the corner of the room where Mary lay with her baby nestled in her arms. "You picked a fine woman there for a wife, I hope you realize that."

James nodded his head as she continued speaking.

"She will be a bit emotional over the next few weeks and that's only natural, so take everything she says with a pinch of salt. If she has a sharp tongue, ignore it. She's a grand girl with a good heart and will be back to her old self in no time. Well, I'm off to my own bed – Pat should have it nice and warm by now." Annie stood up and patted James on the back. "I'm glad you came to stay, it's brought a new lease of life to both of us. If you and Mary decide to join your family in England we would miss you terribly, but you have to do what's best for your child now."

James stood and hugged his aunt. "The thought of going there never entered my head. No matter how bad things get here, this is where I want my family to be reared. I know Mary feels the same way. So we will have no more talk of that. You go on up, Pat will be missing you. I can look after the fire."

Annie smiled at her nephew's words and took one last look at the sleeping baby before climbing the stairs.

After tending the fire, James lay on the other bed in the parlour, looking over at Mary, sleeping peacefully. It was hard to imagine she was the same young woman he had seen writhing in agony earlier that evening.

Sleep did not come to him easily that night. He tossed and turned, drifting in and out of a strange dream about a young girl in prison and Mary standing outside, at a barred window. She had pushed her arms through the gaps, holding onto the child, both of them sobbing their hearts out. James woke up, his body damp with sweat, and looked over at his young family.

"I'm sorry, love, did the baby wake you with her crying?" Mary whispered as she stroked her daughter's head of dark brown hair. "She's so hungry, this is the third time she has suckled since she was born."

James asked if he could lie in beside them and Mary made room for him. As he held them both in his arms an overwhelming sense of responsibility swept through him, and James instinctively knew this feeling would motivate him for the rest of his life.

"She is so beautiful, just like her mother," he said, then added mischievously, "She sounds like you, too."

Slapping him on the leg Mary said, "And that's what she'll get if she is as saucy as you."

She placed the sleeping baby in his arms and asked, "Are we still agreed on calling her Catherine, after my mother?"

James felt a warm glow as he held his daughter for the first time. It was a feeling that would make him agree to anything asked of him.

"Of course," said James, "That's the tradition isn't it? The first boy after the man's father and the first girl after the woman's mother. It's nice that one of my sisters is also called Catherine, in fact, there's lots of Catherine McGrothers in our family. It's a good solid name, one she will be proud to bear when she's older."

CHAPTER FIVE

James could see four boats spread out in the bay, their vessel being last to sail. On board with him was his uncle Pat, along with the owner of the boat and his son. The fishermen called out greetings to each other as they passed. It was midnight. A pale ribbon of moonlight lay over the quiet sea and the air was very still.

"A calm before the storm I would say Tom," remarked Pat. "We will have to head back to shore at the first sign of a breeze."

Tom Matthews looked at his fifteen year old son, Joseph, the only one left of five. Three of his boys had gone to America six months before and one had died of the fever. His wife and two young daughters depended on them catching enough fish tonight to eat for the next week – if they were lucky. The weather being so bad the previous three days, nobody had risked bringing a boat out to sea. As soon as the wind calmed, the fishermen set out, thankful for the opportunity to replenish their depleted food supply. Under normal circumstances none of them would have chanced going out with a storm expected, but times were hard and food scarce.

Mary's eyes were fixed on the boat carrying James away from the shore. In the pale moonlight, she could just make out the shape of her husband, rowing along with one of the other crew. Having gone to bed early, Annie was fast asleep upstairs, blissfully unaware of the fact that both their men were at sea. Mary knew the older woman really did worry, even if she pretended not to. "At least one of us will get some sleep," she whispered to the empty parlour.

As the night wore on, all of the boats landed some fish. Not a huge amount, but enough for their families. A wind began to blow, announcing the impending storm. Pulling up the nets with whatever precious catch was in them, the fishermen hastily made ready to sail back to the safety of the shore. They were a mile out, not wanting to risk going any further on that particular night. The sudden swell of the sea tossing the boats made rowing difficult. James and Tom, being the strongest, took the oars. Pat and Joseph, the oldest and youngest on board, bailed out the water deposited by every wave breaking over them.

"We need to climb on the back of the biggest wave that comes along, James," Tom shouted above the howling wind. "It will carry us to shore if we're lucky."

The young man listened to every instruction that was given him by the older, more experienced sailor. James had been in rough seas before, even as a child, and knew the importance of keeping a level head.

The shrill whistling of the wind through the door broke into Mary's sleep. Her baby was lying at her side, warm and content. Slowly she eased herself off the bed so as not to disturb the sleeping child and took up her watch at the small window. It framed a scene the young woman would remember for the rest of her life. Angry, black clouds raced across a charcoal grey sky. The light from the full moon revealing a boiling sea that, from time to time, threw up into the air small dark shapes. Mary knew those were the boats that had gone out earlier, one of them carrying her husband.

James felt a numbness in his arms, and looked to see if he was holding the oars. He couldn't tell if they were still in his hands, the cold having frozen his fingers around the wood. Tom was shouting words at him, some of which the wind stole away. Others he managed to hear and follow. Pat went very still and was looking past James at something behind him. It seemed like the boat stopped moving for a second, and then they were lifted up as if a giant hand was balancing them on its palm.

Mary could not take her eyes off the scene being played out before her. She focused on one of the boats that had been lifted by a huge wave, heading towards the shore. Praying that James was on it, she held her breath as it got nearer. From nowhere, a bigger wave rose up and swallowed the boat with its crew. Her eyes searched until they hurt, dark clouds obscuring her view. When the moonlight broke through, all that could be seen was the empty, angry sea. Not a boat in sight. Feeling like a knife had been thrust into her heart, Mary ran upstairs to wake up Annie.

Some of the other boats had been lifted along with theirs. James never took his eyes off Tom, waiting for his direction. Timing it as best he could, Tom gave the signal for Pat and Joseph to get behind James, tipping the bow of the boat up into the air. A vessel to their left had reached the top of a nearby wave. Moving forward, gathering speed, it was hit by a huge swell coming in from the side. Just as the sea was engulfing the helpless boat nearby, James and the other fishermen were plunged into darkness. Pat and Joe continued to bail out water in anticipation of taking on more. It seemed like they were flying through the air and James was vaguely aware of other boats alongside them, surging forward, on the crest of the wave.

******

Annie was distraught at what she had been told. The two women clung to each other and cried, until Mary stood back and wiped her tears away.

"Will you keep an eye on Catherine, please? I'll go down to the village and find out what news there is?" Mary drew a blanket around her shoulders before running out into the night.

All but the youngest and oldest villagers had gathered on the beach, watching helplessly as their husbands, sons, fathers and brothers were tossed about by the raging sea. Like a scene from a ballet, the small vessels moved gracefully through the darkness towards the shore, their bows raised into the air. The wave crashed onto the sandy beach, depositing the boats and their crew almost at the feet of the onlookers.

As she approached the crowd of people the sound of wailing and crying reached Mary's ears. She was sure her husband and his uncle had lost their lives. When James called out to her, she didn't respond immediately. It was Pat placing a hand on her arm as she passed him by, that made her realize she was not a widow.

"James, James," she was shouting, pushing her way through the crowd.

"Mary, I'm over here."

The young woman followed the voice of her husband and found him sitting on a seaweed covered rock, coughing and still calling her name.

"We lost a boat and three men. I thought I would never set eyes on you again," James gasped.

They held each other until Pat joined them and helped his nephew to his feet.

"We should get back to Annie, she will be worried sick," the old fisherman said.

The three tired figures made their way to the cottage, but before they reached it the door swung open and Annie ran out, thrusting herself into Pat's arms.

"Calm down, love, you can't get rid of me that easily. Sure how many times have I told you that?" he said, patting her back and kissing her wet cheek.

In the safe, steady, warmth of the cottage the men recounted their story to the women. The baby, who had woken up looking for a feed, was suckled, swaddled, kissed and passed to her father.

"The catch from the four remaining boats will be shared out and an equal portion given to the widows and children of the perished men," said Pat. "That being the case, we should have enough to do us till the weather clears. If you will excuse me, I am going up to bed now. I lost some good friends in that storm, I won't be much company for you tonight."

As he began to climb the stairs, Annie took his hand and said, "I'll come with you, love, we can warm the bed together tonight."

CHAPTER SIX

The families of the drowned fishermen, all female with no man to provide for them, decided to move to Liverpool. One of them had relatives there and was told that a word in the right ear could lead to a job for the women as domestics in some of the big houses. The potato crop had failed again for the second year running and for those who couldn't pay their rent it meant the workhouse or the boat. Most of those leaving the area were heading for Liverpool from Dundalk. It was a sad day for the village when the two widows and their three daughters left.

An older girl, Brigid, who had married the year before and was living with her husband's family, moved into her parent's cottage with permission from the landlord. He had been very sympathetic, providing coffins for the burials of the four men, whose bodies had been washed ashore the day after the storm. Wreckage from their boat had been scattered along the beach and on the rocks.

Brigid's husband, Michael, was also a fisherman and worked on his father's boat. His parents' house was crowded enough already and the young couple were expecting their first child. If they could afford to pay the rent on the cabin it would mean Brigid's family would have a place to come back to if things didn't work out in England. A close friendship had developed between Michael and James and their wives. The two young women spent a lot of time searching through the woods with Annie, learning about the cures she had for different ailments and the plants that were edible or poisonous. In late summer there were wild berries to collect and in the autumn, mushrooms. If they came across a puffball, there was great excitement, it was as good as a piece of meat and made a tasty meal.

It was on one of these walks in October, while carrying her baby and a sack of mushrooms, that Mary heard her friend Brigid call out in distress, some distance behind her. Annie had stayed close to the young, heavily pregnant woman, as both of them were tired and kept the same pace. When Mary reached them, Brigid was lying on a bed of leaves while the older woman examined her swollen belly.

With a worried look on her face, Annie held her arms out to take Mary's baby. "Quickly now, give me Catherine and go fetch Michael. He will have to carry Brigid, it will take her too long to walk back and I think she is very far on in her labour."

Mary knew it would take twenty minutes at least for her to reach the village. She prayed that the baby wouldn't be in too much of a hurry to be born, remembering how quickly she had given birth to Catherine seven months before.

The men were mending their nets in preparation for an evening's fishing. Michael knew by the way Mary ran towards them that something was very wrong. He went to meet her as she slumped to the ground, trying to catch her breath.

"It's Brigid....the baby....coming," she gasped.

Michael shouted back to one of the young boys helping with the nets to run and tell Kitty Carroll. "Bring her to my house so she can get things ready."

"Come on, Mary, show us where she is," said James, lifting his wife up and helping her along.

"Annie is with her, and Catherine too," replied Mary. "We were gathering mushrooms. It came on all of a sudden."

Michael raced ahead of his friends as soon as he heard Brigid's cries coming from deep in the woods. He knelt beside her and Annie told him to wait until the pain had eased before lifting her up.

The older woman looked from Mary to Brigid and shook her head slowly. "I don't know why your babies are in such a rush to get into this world, if they knew the state of it they would stay put."

It was a long contraction and as soon as Annie felt the muscle soften on Brigid's abdomen she instructed Michael to lift her.

They made their way through the trees, the men taking turns in carrying the young woman, not stopping to rest, even when she cried out with each band of pain that tightened around her belly.

Kitty Carroll had the water boiling and clean cloths ready by the time Michael carried Brigid into their home. The men were swept back out through the door to wait, while the women bustled around preparing for the new arrival.

Each cry of pain that his wife let out drew Michael to the door. James had to stop his friend from going in several times. Immediately following a loud scream, the cry of a baby was heard and wild horses could not have dragged the young man back. Michael burst in through the doorway and sat at Brigid's side, kissing her brow and telling her how brave she was. Annie was cleaning the baby and swaddling it in a blanket.

She handed the newborn infant to Michael saying, "Look at the head of black hair on him. There's no mistaking whose son he is."

The young father beamed. "A boy, Brigid, well done. We should call him Francis, after your father. Your mother will like that. We can call the next one after mine."

The baby started to wriggle and squirm and Michael handed him to Brigid. "I think he wants a feed, love," he said.

Annie grabbed Michael by the arm and pulled him up, dragging him towards the door. "Your poor wife has been through enough without you planning on the next child already. Off you go to Paddy Mac's and wet the baby's head. This isn't the time to have a man about, under our feet. Away with you now," and the young father was pushed through the door.

"I have a son, James. A fine, healthy son."

"By the sound of his wail, he has a fine pair of lungs, Michael, that's for sure," laughed James.

"The women have thrown me out of my own house to go wet the baby's head. Mind you, it will be a cup of tea we'll be getting at Paddy Mac's – if we are lucky, that is," Michael grumbled. "After a second year of blight there's nothing to make any poitín from."

"Ah would you stop your whining. We are bound to get a drop of porter at least. Sure Paddy Mac is only too happy to have the promise of some fish in exchange for his drink," said James.

The two young men set out to celebrate, determined to push as far away as possible the worries that came with fatherhood – at least for one evening. It was a good thing they could not see what the months ahead would bring.

CHAPTER SEVEN

The winter of 1846 was particularly harsh due to another failure of the potato crop. A relief committee had been established in the parish in October of that year. Local contributions and government grants supported schemes like road works, mostly employing women, young children and the elderly, who were deemed unsuitable for working the land. Pat and James had stored up enough salted herring to see them through the winter. They even had a couple of hens left, having sold some to pay their rent the month before.

"There's talk of men earning up to four shillings a day, in England," said Michael, who had called to see James one evening.

"That's only the navvies, they are seasoned workers. You would be lucky if you got half that, son," Pat said.

Mary shook her finger at Michael saying. "So you are the one putting ideas of leaving us into my husband's head."

"Now that's not fair," said James, "I was the one who suggested it when the blight struck again this year. Michael is right to think about it. Half the county are heading over to Liverpool, in fact, whole families are going."

There was a heavy silence in the room as everyone stared into the fire and thought about what had been said. The only sound to be heard was the hissing of steam from the burning damp turf.

"What does Brigid say about it, Michael?" Mary asked.

"She says she would go with me if we didn't have Francis, but she won't bring him because of the disease and fever that's raging over there."

"I wouldn't want you and Catherine to risk it either, Mary," James said. "If we go it will only be for a few months in the spring. We would need to be back here for the summer to fish and cut the turf. Pat's getting too old to do all that now."

"I was thinking of going with you, it might be nice to go to bed and not have someone climb in and take all the heat from me," the older man laughed.

Annie slapped him on the leg and laughed back. "If you go over there, old man, chances are you will end up sleeping in the gutter, and there'll be plenty wanting to climb in with you – and I'm not talking about people."

Mary was upset and did not try to hide how she felt. "I don't want you to go, we can manage until the summer can't we?"

It was obvious to everyone in the room that the two young men were serious about leaving. James agreed they could probably feed themselves for the winter but asked if anyone knew how they would get money to pay the rent. Michael was already a month behind.

"We could sell something, my lovely wooden bowls might fetch a good price," offered Annie.

"When that money is gone what would we do?" asked James. "It's no good putting off what needs to be done. The fares are so low now, we should take advantage of it. If we don't get work in Liverpool then we can go on to Durham and stay with my family. There are plenty of McGrothers there now."

James had given it a lot of thought and was prepared to do whatever it took to keep a roof over their heads. Mary wanted to know how he was going to raise the money for the journey.

"Michael and myself have been talking about this for a while, now. The worst of the weather will be behind us by the time March comes in, and we can sell or pawn our heavy coats, we won't need them by then."

As it turned out, nobody had to sell their coat because the landlord had some ditches that needed digging and the two young fishermen earned their fare with enough left over to cover at least a month's rent. Mary and Brigid tried to talk them out of leaving when March came round, but it was no use, their minds were made up.

A month before Catherine's first birthday, James and Michael bought the tickets. With heavy hearts the men said goodbye to their wives at the quays in Dundalk. The babies had been left in the care of Annie and Pat, while the couples walked the two miles into the town.

"Don't stand close to anyone coughing or sweating. Do you hear me, both of you?" Mary cautioned.

"That might be difficult, look at the crowds waiting to board," said Michael apprehensively, uneasy himself about the journey.

James drew his wife into his arms, murmuring, "Is this too close?" and kissed her.

"This is definitely too close for anyone but me, sick or not," she said.

Mary was trying to keep a smile on her face but her heart felt heavy and ached. She didn't want her husband to remember her frowning and upset as he sailed away. Looking over at Brigid, who was crying, Mary could see that Michael was having difficulty in consoling his young wife.

"I'm not sure I want to watch you both leave, it might be better to say our goodbyes here. What do you say Brigid?" Mary called out to her friend.

James was about to disagree. He wanted to watch his wife as he left the shore and drink in every last detail of her until she disappeared from his sight, but he knew she was trying to make it easier for Brigid.

Instead he agreed with the suggestion. "That's the best thing to do, Mary. It will be hard for the two of us sailing away from the both of ye. Better for you to be leaving us. What do you think, Michael?"

His friend nodded in agreement. As Brigid held on tightly to him, Michael kissed her, promising that everything would be alright and they would be home in no time.

"I will be watching from the house, you know that don't you," whispered Mary, not wanting to pull herself out of her husband's arms.

James brushed her forehead with his lips. "I know, love. I will be standing on the deck looking back until I cannot see land anymore."

Having said their goodbyes, the two young women walked away, turning every few steps to wave and blow kisses to their men.

"Stop snivelling and give Michael a smile, Brigid. Do you want him to remember his wife with swollen red eyes and a snotty nose?"

Mary knew she was being harsh but it needed to be said.

There was a loud sigh and a sniff, then Brigid straightened up her shoulders and turned around, putting a brave smile on her face as she joined her friend in blowing one last kiss towards the young men standing on the quayside.

James watched as they rounded a corner and disappeared. A sharp pain went through him as the memory of waving goodbye to his brothers and sisters on the road from Monaghan, only a little over a year before, came flooding back.

CHAPTER EIGHT

The crossing was rough for most of the people on board, but not for James and Michael, who were seasoned fishermen. The young men tried not to look at the dreadful state many of the children were in. There was nothing they could do and it made them realize how lucky they were to still have a roof over their heads. One little girl in particular caught Michael's eye. He pointed her out to James.

"She looks a bit like Catherine, doesn't she?" he said.

"Too much like her. If we don't find work our own families could end up on a boat like this and in the same condition," said James sadly.

"Don't be thinking like that, as long as we can come up with the rent, they will be fine. Pat and Annie will make sure there's food to keep them all going till we get back."

Michael took from his pocket one of the flat cakes of meal Annie had prepared for their journey, handing it to the small child. She looked sickly and frail but when her older brother tried to grab it she hid the food under her armpit, holding on tight. No amount of tugging on his part could dislodge her hand. James stepped forward with another cake, holding it out to the boy, who looked to be four years old. His mother smiled, thanking them for their kindness.

"Do ye have children yourselves?" she asked.

The men nodded and told her they were travelling alone to Liverpool to look for work.

"Be very careful who you trust over there," she looked around, lowering her voice. "Just because someone is a fellow Irishman doesn't mean they won't cheat you. Make sure you see your lodgings before you hand over any money. My husband has been working in Liverpool for the past six months so I know what I'm talking about. The first day he arrived he ended up in a stinking wet cellar on Scotland Road. He had paid a week's rent and couldn't get his money back. In the short time he was there, three people died of the fever. He came back from work one day and sat down on a bench to rest, talking to the man beside him. When he got no answer, my husband nudged him and the poor unfortunate just keeled over. Stone dead he was," the woman made the sign of a cross as did the two young men. "That was on the fifth day, two others having died the night before. My man got himself out of there fast, even though he had two days left on his rent."

James offered her one of his cakes but she shook her head.

"I best not, I don't feel too well and it would be an awful waste to throw good food up over the side, wouldn't it?"

Michael stepped back pulling James with him which made her laugh.

"Don't worry, it's not the fever. I'm just seasick. My husband fished for years and brought me out on occasion, when the sea was calm. It didn't make any difference." She pointed to a line of people leaning over the side and emptying what little there was in their stomachs into the choppy sea. "At least I'm not as bad as that. Maybe it's because I have these two wee ones to care for and can't afford to be ailing."

"Thanks for the advice about the lodgings, did your husband find a decent place in the end?" asked James.

"He did, or we wouldn't be joining him. Avoid the Scotland and Vauxhall Road areas. They are the worst, with more disease and poverty packed into one place than you ever saw in your life. Anywhere outside of those would be safe enough. We are going to share a small house with my husband's cousin and his family. In time we should be able to get a place of our own. Getting some schooling for the children is important too, would you not agree?"

James smiled as he replied, "My father went to a hedge school and told me he was always freezing in the winter, having to learn to read and write in a ditch. When a school was permitted to open only a mile from our house, he made sure myself and my sisters attended. My older brothers were all working so I was the only son in our family that got an education. Even after the death of our parents, when I was very young, my sisters dragged me to school with them. As soon as I reached the age of ten I put my foot down and refused to go. I told them I was ready to work in the fields alongside the other men. I'm sorry now I didn't stay a bit longer – it would have made me a better reader."

"Figures are what's important, never mind letters. You can put a cross where your name needs to go but if you can't count your change then you're in big trouble," Michael said.

"I suppose you're right about that. Neither myself nor my husband can read or write but nobody can short change us, that's for sure," agreed the woman.

Someone shouted they could see land and James and Michael, excusing themselves, went to the bow to get a glimpse of their destination.

Sailing into such a huge port full of ships and boats of all shapes and sizes was overwhelming for the two young men. Their eyes darted from one thing to another as they nudged elbows and pointed fingers at each new sight. It took a few minutes for James to actually see the people teeming on the docks like ants.

"Have you ever seen that many people in one place before, Michael?" he asked.

"As a matter of fact I have – even more. Daniel O'Connell came to Dundalk about five years ago. New Year's Day, 1842, to be exact. I thought I would never in my life see a bigger crowd than the one that gathered for that. Sixty or seventy thousand turned up."

"I can't imagine a bigger crowd than that," James said, looking down on the people bustling around the quay as their boat docked.

"I can, easily," replied Michael feeling like a man of the world. "In June of the following year he came to Castletown and my father brought me there to hear him speak. They say he spoke to a gathering of three hundred thousand that day, me included."

James was impressed, this was a side of his friend he hadn't seen before.

"So you will be well used to making your way through a crowd. I don't need to worry about us getting lost or robbed, do I?"

Michael laughed at that, "As long as I'm sober, we'll be fine. Just don't let me drink too much, I can't handle it. My father practically carried me the two miles home from Dundalk the first time we heard O'Connell speak. I was only seventeen and it being New Year's Day as well, sure the drink was flowing, though mostly among the younger men."

Before anyone could leave the boat James saw two men come on board. One of them carried a black doctor's bag and went below deck with some of the crew. A little while later three bodies were brought up. The anxious crowd, waiting to disembark, separated to form a passageway allowing the stretcher bearers to pass through. As a heavy silence hung in the air, James became aware of the different sounds coming from the docks below; horses, people, the squeak of pulleys hoisting cargo. It seemed like he was in the middle of a dream as he watched the stretchers move slowly past him.

The silence was suddenly cut with a cry he had heard before. It was the same sound Mary had made when she saw her mother's body on the cart. A shiver went down his spine as the doctor came up on deck and stood to one side of the gangplank, calling forward the crew carrying one last stretcher. On it were two tiny bodies wrapped in white sheets. James gasped as he saw a small flat cake, grasped tight by a little hand, sticking out from beneath one of the covers. Two women followed the stretcher, sobbing and holding onto each other, a young boy between them trying to keep up, buried in their skirts. Both men recognized the woman they had been speaking with earlier.

A lump like a rock had formed in James's throat, as he fought back tears, thinking of his own daughter and how vulnerable she was.

"Are you alright?" Michael asked.

James nodded, forcing himself to swallow. "I was thinking of Catherine. I can't imagine what that little girl's father will feel like when he finds out. It would kill me."

"Do you think it was the fever, or the hunger?" asked Michael.

James sighed deeply. "Both," he said, "If there was no starvation there would be no fever. She wouldn't even be on this crowded vessel if her father could have stayed at home."

Nobody was allowed onshore until the doctor had examined their throats. One by one, the passengers filed past him as he looked into their mouths. Every now and again someone would have to stand to one side, denied permission to leave the boat. James and Michael stepped ashore, joining the crowd of hungry, ragged people who had crossed the Irish Sea hoping for something better. For some, that did happen, but for others it was a case of out of the frying pan and into the fire.

CHAPTER NINE

What had been a constant drizzle became a heavy downpour. James and Michael found themselves taking shelter in an overcrowded, derelict building. Babies were crying and elderly men and women lay on the damp floor, too exhausted to sit upright. The wind forced the rain in through the empty door and window frames and people huddled together, trying to stay dry. A young couple sat on the floor, their backs against the cold stone wall, with a small child on each lap. Their clothing was thin and ragged and James was troubled by the sight of the young children shivering. He removed his coat, handing it to the father.

"Wrap this around your family it will help keep them warm. I can share my friend's coat."

As he sat on the floor, James put his hands over his face, trying to block out the misery surrounding him.

"You can't help everyone. In the end all we can do is help ourselves. What good will it do your family if you get sick? How are you going to stay warm now?" asked Michael, taking his coat off to share it with James.

"I know, I know. It just isn't possible to see all this suffering and not be affected by it. How do you do it, Michael?"

"Do you think I don't care? Of course I do, but I have my own family to think of. They are depending on me to provide for them. They will end up in the workhouse if anything happens to me. So *I* can't afford the luxury of sympathy right now, James, and *you* need to toughen up or you'll be no good to anybody."

This was the first time Michael had ever felt anger towards his friend.

"Pat and Annie will look after our families, they promised," said James.

"Your uncle is a fisherman, how many of his friends have drowned over the years? It could be his turn next," said Michael.

James grabbed his friend by the neck of his shirt and pulled his face close. "Don't even think that. You should know better than to tempt fate," he said, fighting the urge to throw a punch.

Realizing he had gone too far, James released his grip and Michael moved away, letting his coat slip down onto the damp floor. An uncomfortable silence filled the gap between them until James put out his hand and asked to be forgiven for the harsh words he had spoken. After a few seconds, Michael smiled and firmly shook his hand.

"We are both tired and hungry. Apology accepted."

The coat was pulled up and the two young men tried to get whatever sleep they could, under the circumstances.

As the weak light of morning crept into the building, people stood up stiffly and stretched. The young father approached James holding out his coat.

"Thank you for your kindness," he said.

"I think you should keep it, for your children," James replied.

"They won't need it where they are going. The workhouse provides clothing as well as shelter. It's just a temporary measure until I get work. These derelict buildings breed disease. My family will be better off there for a while."

He walked back to his wife, lifted up the smallest child, and took hold of the other little one's hand. The young family walked out into the cold, morning air without a backward glance.

"At least you got your coat back," Michael said.

Thousands of Irish were pouring into Liverpool. Many had just walked away from their homes, with nothing left to lose. Others had been evicted, sometimes having their passage paid by landlords anxious to clear their land of tenants who couldn't keep up with the rent. Some headed for Liverpool in the hopes of earning enough money there to take them on to America. Often they never made it out of Liverpool, even when they found work. All their money went on lodgings and food, with nothing left to save.

"When will Brigid's mother and the girls be finished work?" asked James.

They had arranged to meet up with them in a park later that day.

"They have every Sunday afternoon off and when the weather is dry they get together for a walk in the fresh air," Michael sniffed. "Not that you would call this fresh."

Having walked for hours around the city the young men realized how difficult it would be for them to find any kind of permanent work. Anyone they spoke to advised them to move on or go home. Quite a few said Manchester was promising. James and Michael talked it over while sitting in the park, waiting for the women to show up. By the time they had arrived the decision had been made to move on to Durham and join James's family.

Brigid's sisters and her mother had brought jars of tea wrapped in a cloth, fresh bread, boiled beef and some cake with them.

"One of the cooks took pity on ye when we told her who we were meeting," Michael's mother-in-law said.

"Tell her she's an angel," said James. "This is a banquet."

The two men ate hungrily, but the women would only have tea, advising them to spare out the food and make it last for a day or two. James agreed, though Michael wanted to wolf down the lot. Brigid's mother wrapped up what was left of the meal in the cloth and handed it to James. She took a key from her pocket and put it in Michael's hand.

"The gardener is away until tomorrow morning and he is the only person who would use this key. There is a shed against the back wall of the garden, in among the shrubs. When it gets dark, climb over and let yourselves in. You will have to be gone by six in the morning, but don't worry as I am up from half past five. I can easily slip out and wake you."

Brigid's youngest sister had become very friendly with the son of a barge owner. She had arranged some work for them loading cargo but it was only for a day.

"Anything is welcome, there's no work to be had here," said James.

He told them of their decision to join his brothers in Durham, as they might have better luck there. Brigid's mother was glad to hear it, assuring the young men that as long as they were with family things would work out. That had been the case with her own girls. Every Sunday they all got to see each other and it eased the homesickness for them.

As the evening began to draw in, James suggested they walk the women home. Michael linked his mother-in-law, telling her all about her grandson and what a good mother Brigid was.

"Annie and Pat are looking out for them, so you mustn't worry and when I manage to get some work we won't have any problem paying the rent. The house will be waiting for you when you return home."

Having said their goodbyes, the men took a walk down by the docks to pass the time, until they could sneak into the shed. The lights and laughter of the taverns drew them to look in through the windows, but they had no money to waste on drink. Women came up to the young men offering to show them around and give them a good time, asking if they had just come off the boats. Michael stared at them with his mouth open, amazed at their forwardness.

James pulled him away chiding, "Stop drooling, you're a married man."

"I know, and none of them are a patch on my Brigid, are they?" Michael said, proudly.

"Nor on Mary," said James, still pulling his friend by the arm. "Let's get back to our little shed, we have an early start in the morning."

Before sunrise, a tapping on the door woke James and he turned the key in the lock. Brigid's mother greeted them as she stepped inside.

"Michael, get up. You will have to leave now in case the gardener decides to start earlier than usual. I could lose my job over this."

"We know, you took a big risk and we are very grateful," James said.

Michael kissed her on the cheek and wished her a good morning. His mother-in-law grabbed hold of his hand and pressed some coins wrapped in a piece of paper, into his palm. Both men began to protest.

"Me and the girls want you both to have this. I didn't give it to ye last night in case ye might be tempted to have a drink. The taverns here are not exactly Paddy Mac's now, are they? Have you seen the women who drink in them?"

James and Michael exchanged glances as Brigid's mother swept past, urging them to hurry up and climb over the wall.

"Don't throw away the paper, the name of the barge owner is on it, just show it to one of the shopkeepers near the canal and they will tell you where he is docked. He will be expecting you."

Hugging her one last time, they disappeared over the wall, as she wiped a stream of hot, salty tears from her face, before turning back towards the big house.

CHAPTER TEN

The owner of the barge was happy to have two strong, young men to help him, being short-handed that day. James shook hands with the man and enquired as to when they should start.

"Right away," he said. "See that cart full of sacks of cotton over yonder? They need to be loaded on my barge."

Michael and James had removed their coats even before the sentence was finished.

"Well, that's what I like to see, a bit of enthusiasm," said Matthew, the barge owner.

He gave them instructions as to how the sacks should be stacked and covered, then watched for a while to make sure it was done correctly.

"You look quite capable of managing that on your own, if you need me I will be doing a bit of business in The Grape over there." He pointed to a tavern near the lock and walked towards it.

The young men enjoyed the work and by midday the cargo was loaded. Impressed with their speed and teamwork, Matthew asked if they would like to make the trip to Leeds and back. He had a consignment of coal to collect on his return to Liverpool.

"Is Leeds near Sunderland, by any chance?" asked James.

"A lot nearer than here, that's for sure. Why do you ask?"

"I have family there and we want to join them if we cannot get regular work here. We can load up the coal for you in Leeds, if that's any help," offered James.

Matthew thought for a moment. "I wish I could give you something more permanent but my son needs the work, it's him and his cousin you are filling in for today. But at least you can get the transport and earn a little money on the trip. I will even throw in your meals, how does that sound to you?"

The young men beamed and thanked him for the offer.

Because James had grown up on a farm, he was well able to help out with the horse that pulled the barge. The hot food gave the hungry young men a boost of energy that kept them working all day. No job was too difficult for them, even repairing some damage that had been done to the barge, a task that the owner's son had begun but never finished. Matthew was impressed and said so.

"We're both fishermen, well used to looking after a boat," James explained.

Matthew still had to do most of the work with the horse, knowing the canal and its difficult areas, but the two young men were quick learners and made the journey much easier for him. They even insisted on sleeping with the cargo to guard it during the night.

Matthew had a collie that would wake them if anyone even walked past the barge.

"One of you could sleep in my son's bunk. Why not take turns on watch?" Matthew suggested.

James offered to sleep up top for the first night so Michael went below, glad to have a bed to sleep in for the first time since leaving home. Matthew went to an Inn for a nightcap and when he came back he had a young woman on each arm. The trio looked at the sleeping James and one of the women nudged him with her foot but he just grunted and turned over.

Early next morning, half asleep with his eyes closed, James smiled as he stroked the soft, long hair belonging to the warm body lying beside him.

"Mary," he murmured as he slowly woke up.

A roar of laughter from Michael jolted him out of his slumber. When James opened his eyes the collie was licking his face.

"So that's how Mary wakes you up in the morning. She could teach Brigid a thing or two."

A young woman brushed past Michael and stepped off the barge, blowing a kiss back to Matthew.

"Where did she come from?" asked James, wiping his face.

Matthew smiled and said, "We have an arrangement. In fact her friend came back here with us last night but you were out cold, James. Some watchman you are, and Michael couldn't be woken either. Not that we tried too hard, both of you being married, you probably wouldn't have been interested, would you?"

The young men shook their heads vigorously.

"Would that have come out of our wages, Matthew?" asked Michael.

The barge owner shook with laughter. "Of course it would. All I'm providing is bed and board and a hot meal."

"Thanks for thinking of us," said James, "But you are widowed and entitled to have an *arrangement*.' It wouldn't be right for either of us. I'm glad we slept. We might have been tempted."

"I know, lad, the girls talked me into it. The other one went off with a man she knew, who happened to be passing by."

CHAPTER ELEVEN

Having helped to load the coal on the barge, James and Michael bade farewell and thanked Matthew for getting them to Leeds.

"Look me up next time you are in Liverpool," he shouted back, as he set off to retrieve his horse from the stable in which it had spent the night.

A young man who had been glad of a lift to Liverpool, was on the barge unravelling ropes that would be needed for the journey. He warned the two Irishmen to be careful of where they slept and ate as there was typhus in the city, especially the east side, called the Bank. This was where many who had tried to escape the poverty and hunger in Ireland had ended up. It was a place they should avoid at all cost.

"Shouldn't we just keep walking and head for Sunderland?" Michael suggested as they looked around the streets.

James knew that would be the sensible thing to do. "Matthew did say it would only take a couple of days to walk it," he said, "Let's buy some bread and ask someone to point us in the right direction."

A young girl was begging outside a shop as James and Michael went inside. They purchased some food and asked the grocer which of the streets would lead them to the road for Sunderland. Giving them directions, he stepped outside.

"Go on with you," he shouted at the frail little thing standing at his door, hands outstretched.

"Pesky beggars" he said as they watched her shuffle up the street and turn into an alley.

As James and Michael approached the spot where the young girl had disappeared, a pair of small, grubby feet could be seen on the ground sticking out from the laneway. James ran ahead to look around the corner and found her lying in the dirt crying, pitiful sobs shaking her tiny frame.

He gently picked up the child, asking where she lived. She was as light as a feather and cold as ice.

"Cross Street," she said weakly. "Do you know the Bank?"

"If I carry you can you show us the way? Will your mother be home?" asked James.

The little girl shook her head.

"My mammy died last week. My daddy will be there."

Pleading with James to leave the child make her own way home, Michael followed, at a distance.

Standing in front of the house the young girl had brought them to, James and Michael had to hold their noses to avoid the stench. They gave her some of the bread they had bought and watched as she ran inside, her bare feet ankle-deep in muck. Both men turned quickly and ran from the area, not

71

stopping until they were sure the squalor and stench was far behind. Walking in silence, Michael didn't know whether to be angry with his friend or proud of him.

After a day and a half's walk, taking only short breaks to rest, James was exhausted and suggested they look for somewhere to spend the night. Finding a field through which a clear, stream flowed, the young men decided it was a good place to get some sleep. There was a small copse of trees at the water's edge and if it rained at least it would afford some shelter. Night was falling fast, bringing with it a cold breeze. Michael was shivering with the drop in temperature as he watched his friend sleep. There was something different about James. He was shivering too, but there were beads of sweat on his forehead.

"James, James, wake up." Michael was worried.

"I c..c..can't st..stop sha..k...king," James was drenched.

"You have a fever. Could you walk if I helped you? We need to get to your family."

Michael took hold of his friend's hand and pulled. James tried to stand but slumped to the ground within seconds. There was only one thing to do. Taking his coat off, Michael carefully placed it over James, saying he would go find his brothers and bring them back with him. Filling the jar his mother-in-law had given them with water from the stream, Michael set it beside James and placed a wet cloth across his forehead.

"Keep sipping the water, I won't be long. Nobody would give us a ride with you as sick as you are, but I might get one on my own. I promise, James, I'll be back soon, even if I have to run all the way."

Michael ran through the night, until he got a lift on a cart, having promised to help unload it. Following the directions given him by the carter, Michael found the street that the McGrother families lived on. It was still dark as he knocked loudly on the first door he came to. A sleepy old man appeared, a worried look on his face.

"Where's the fire, son? What has you calling at this hour of the night?"

"Please, mister... tell me which house... the McGrothers live in. Their brother... needs help." Michael could hardly breathe, having run non-stop for almost an hour. He was bent over, hands on his knees taking in huge gulps of air.

The old man crossed the street and banged on a door. Michael recognized Owen as soon as he laid eyes on him.

"James is sick, I left him to rest while I ran on ahead. Can you get a cart? We could be there in a few hours with a horse."

Everyone sprung into action. Owen's wife, Rose, gathered whatever blankets could be spared from her relatives. Someone arrived at the top of the street with a horse and cart and Owen and his wife, along with Michael, climbed onto it. The carter gave the reins to Owen and jumped down, saying the horse would get there quicker with less weight to pull.

As they travelled through the night, Michael told them about the young girl James had carried and how they had run from the squalor she was living in.

"I think he picked up the fever from her," he said.

"Typhus doesn't come on that quick, it would take at least a week. Did you sleep in a crowded place when you arrived in Liverpool or were you kept below deck on the way over?" asked Rose.

"We stayed above deck all the way over, but some people died on the journey. A doctor looked in our mouths before we were allowed off the boat." Then Michael remembered something. "We spent the first night in Liverpool in a crowded ruin of a place because the weather was so bad. James gave his coat to a young family whose children were shivering with the cold. The father gave it back to him next morning."

"I don't think it was just the cold making them shiver. It might have been the fever," Owen said.

It wasn't long before Michael saw the copse of trees and Owen reined in the horse. As the cart came to a halt Michael jumped down and Rose handed him the blankets, along with a bag containing herbs and medicine. The two of them climbed over the fence and raced up the field, while the horse was being tethered.

"James, I'm back. Owen and Rose are with me," shouted Michael running towards his friend, who was sitting up resting against a tree.

There was a strange look in James's eyes and he was beating the ground around him with a stick. Michael tried to coax him into drinking some water.

"He's delirious," said Rose standing at a distance. "James, we need to put you in the stream, do you understand what I'm saying?" she shouted.

Still brandishing the stick, James looked at his sister-in-law and cried out, "Mary, get back. The dogs will eat you, they're hungry, go home, love. Take care of Catherine."

Owen stepped forward to go to his brother but Rose put her arm across his chest, stopping him in his tracks.

"Don't touch him yet. Take off all your clothes. Michael you can leave yours on. You are going to bring James to the stream and hold him down."

"Am I to get into the water fully dressed?" asked Michael.

"It looks like typhus, which is spread by lice," said Rose, "So James and his clothes are probably crawling with them. You may have picked up some yourself. Everything you are wearing will need to be boiled, but for now, dunking will have to do."

Owen was already naked, kneeling down beside his youngest brother, having left his clothes in a pile near the cart. Michael helped him remove his friend's clothing, which was damp with sweat.

The two men carried James, who was still lashing out at something only he could see. He screamed when they put him into the cold water and it took all their strength to hold him down. Michael freed the stick from his clenched fist and after a few minutes, James's body relaxed as he passed out. Rose gave them the soap she had brought with her and they laid him on the grass to wash him down.

Wrapped in blankets and carried back to the cart, James seemed to be in a restful sleep, in spite of having a rasping cough. Owen picked up his brother's clothes and held them under the cold water for a few minutes and Rose urged the men to wash themselves with the soap, as a precaution.

"Come on Michael, let's make sure we don't bring any unwelcome guests back with us," said Owen.

He stood on the grassy bank and lathered his body, while Michael looked on shivering, still in his wet clothes.

"What's wrong with you, man? Strip off and soap up."

The young man turned his head to look at the cart. Realizing that Michael was too embarrassed to stand naked in front of a woman, Owen tried not to laugh.

"Don't mind our Rose, she works at the infirmary. There's nothing she hasn't seen, Michael. Besides, she's too busy caring for James to be bothered looking at you – and me she can see anytime," said Owen, throwing the soap.

Michael caught it and laughed. "I suppose you're right," he said, peeling off his drenched clothing.

Owen jumped into the stream to rinse off. Before getting dressed, he gathered the wet clothes belonging to James and Michael and tied them into a bundle to hang off the cart. Rose said she would boil them when they got home. The sun was beginning to rise but the air was chilly and Michael shivered, glad of the blanket he had been given.

"How are you feeling yourself?" Rose asked.

The young man shrugged his shoulders, "Hungry and cold, but not sick."

"You should be alright so. But let me know the minute you feel unwell," said Rose.

Michael nodded and looked at James, who was deathly pale. Rose could see how anxious he was about his friend and felt the need to reassure him.

"He's as strong as a horse, always has been. Don't worry about him. One of the doctors gave me some medicine they use in the infirmary so I could look after a sick neighbour. I still have plenty left. Anyway, not everyone dies from typhus, you know. It's mostly the old, the very young and those suffering from starvation that do. A weakened body finds it hard to fight off disease."

Rose gave Michael another blanket as he was still shivering. The journey back home was a quiet one, with everyone too exhausted to make any attempt at conversation.

CHAPTER TWELVE

Rose was sure that James would need to be hospitalized and said so to her husband on the journey home. Owen remained silent for a few minutes, then asked her if they would take him in at the infirmary where she worked.

"Doctor Henshaw will know what's best. I can't say for sure, but if it's typhus he might suggest the workhouse. They have a fever ward," Rose was preparing him for the worst possible news.

"The infirmary has a fever ward too, he can go there," said Owen.

Rose put a hand on his arm, explaining, "It's full to the brim, love. The sick are lying on the floor as it is. I just want you to know what might be said."

"Nobody belonging to me is going into the workhouse. I will find a place to keep him until he's recovered. I can take the time off work. We can manage," Owen meant what he said and there would be no changing his mind.

James started to cough and tried to sit up. "You are not losing your wages on account of me, I'm feeling much better – in spite of the fact that you tried to drown me. I don't recall much of what happened since Michael left me, but I distinctly remember being plunged into freezing cold water."

Rose asked him how long he had been awake and James said he heard her mention typhus.

"Do you think that's what I have?"

"Maybe, I don't know for sure but that's why we dunked you and your clothes in the river, James," his sister-in-law replied.

It wasn't long before the horse turned into Chester Lane, stopping at the infirmary. They had reached their destination.

Rose jumped down from the cart as it pulled up, and ran inside. Owen followed carrying his brother, who was beginning to burn up again, leaving Michael to look after the horse. Instructing them to follow him into an examination room, Doctor Henshaw took one look at the way James was breathing and said he didn't think it was typhus. He checked for the tell-tale rash on his body and other symptoms that would suggest the dreaded disease, some called, the Irish Fever.

There was an epidemic of typhus in 1847 following the mass migration of starving, impoverished people from Ireland to England, America and Canada.

After a thorough examination the doctor informed James that he was suffering from pneumonia. Owen smiled and slapped his brother on the back, which set off another fit of coughing.

Rose gasped and said, "We put him in a stream and then lathered him with soap. I was afraid he would infect us. Did we make him worse?" She knew how serious an illness pneumonia was.

Doctor Henshaw put a hand on her shoulder. "Not at all, Rose. That's what brought his temperature down, but he does need to keep warm."

He gave her instructions on how to care for James, most of which she already knew.

A lot of people had gathered in the street to await the return of the cart. Rose cautioned James to avoid coughing, so as not to alarm anyone, so he closed his eyes, pretending to be asleep. A hush came over the crowd as James was carried by Owen into the house. Michael followed, embarrassed to be among so many strangers wearing only a blanket. Everyone moved away, fearing the worst at the sight of the unconscious young man.

"Is it the fever?" someone asked.

Rose told them that he had pneumonia, not the fever, and had been seen by a doctor.

"He should be in the infirmary, it's wrong of you to bring sickness into our street, Owen, even if it is your brother," a woman shouted out.

"How do we know what you say is the truth?" a voice at the back of the crowd piped up.

Rose turned to face her neighbours before entering the house.

"How many of you have been nursed through an illness by me?" she asked.

An uneasy silence hung in the air.

"Did I ever turn anyone away from my door? There is no need to worry. If I am prepared to let James into my home with my children inside, then you should not be afraid to have him in the street. Nobody is asking you to pay him a visit. Now go back about your business and let us get on with ours."

With that, Rose went inside and slammed the door shut with such force, it made those who were standing nearby jump.

James had been placed upstairs in the children's bed. He was to have that room to himself for the next few weeks. Rose sat by the range and pulled her youngest son up onto her lap.

"No need to be so glum, Jamie," she said, "Your uncle James will be right as rain in no time."

Owen sat beside her, warming himself by the fire. "It's been a long time since I ran naked through a field, Rosie love. Not a very pleasant thing to do at this time of year. I might get sick myself, then you'll have to nurse me, too."

He pulled her close, a strong arm circling her waist.

"You've never been a day sick in your life, Owen McGrother," Rose said, as she tickled the little boy on her knee. "Your daddy is just looking to skive off work, isn't he?"

As young Jamie squirmed and laughed, the memory of the twin daughters they lost to measles just a few years before came flooding back to Owen.

"The doctor is right about the pneumonia, isn't he? I meant what I said earlier about staying somewhere with James until he gets better," he said solemnly.

Rose took his big, calloused hand in hers. She traced every scar with her finger, reminding herself of how hard he worked at the forge to keep them warm and fed. Owen was the eldest in his family and sixteen years older than James. He had been like a father to his youngest brother since the death of their parents. Rose knew what the young man meant to her husband.

"If I felt our children were in any danger I would never have put your brother in their room. They will be sharing with us anyway, and your sister Maggie will be here when I'm at work during the day – to make sure this young scallywag doesn't get in to disturb his uncle."

Again, she tickled her son before allowing him to wriggle free. Owen remarked that the neighbours were not too happy about the situation.

"Never mind that lot, a person can't even have an innocent sneeze without them going into a panic," said Rose.

She stood up and began to prepare breakfast. Michael, who had fallen asleep on a bench against the wall, was snoring loudly.

"I'm glad *he's* staying with Maggie. That noise would wake the dead," she laughed.

CHAPTER THIRTEEN

A loud knock woke Catherine from her afternoon nap and Mary ran to the door, annoyed at whoever was interrupting her daughter's sleep. On the doorstep stood one of Paddy Mac's children.

"Mary – sorry, I mean Mrs. McGrother – can you come to our house, Mammy has news for you. She says you're not to worry, but it's about your husband."

There was a loud screech out of the startled baby as Mary grabbed her from a warm bed. The young boy put his hands over his ears.

"She sure can make a noise, can't she?" he said.

Catherine screamed the whole way to Paddy Mac's. His wife, Bridie, took the baby from Mary and gave her to their eldest daughter to bring outside.

"Show her the hens. That will distract her and mind you keep the shawl around the two of you. There's a bitter wind out there."

Mary stood by the fire, her back to Bridie, preparing herself for the worst.

"Turn around now, girl, and face me. I know what you're thinking, and I'm going to be honest with you. We got a message from a man passing through on his way back from Sunderland. He was asked by a Rose McGrother to call with news of James. Here, sit yourself down," she said pointing to a bench.

Mary shook her head and remained standing.

"Bridie, just tell me, for pity's sake, and put me out of my misery."

"James has pneumonia. His brother's wife, Rose, works at the infirmary near where they live and she has medicine. A doctor has examined him, so he is being well looked after."

Bridie had made some tea and she sat down, patting the space beside her. "Come on now. Have a wee sup, it will make you feel better."

Mary took the cup being held out to her, but instead of sitting, she paced up and down the room, asking what else had been said.

Bridie sighed, "James didn't want you to be told of his illness. He knows you would want to go to him if you found out. Rose asked this man to call. She said if it was her husband, she would want to know. That's the message that was delivered to me."

Mary ran outside, having thanked Bridie for the tea and the news about James. The children were playing with Catherine and making her laugh, but she began to cry again when her mother took her away. Holding her baby close, Mary walked to Brigid's house, deep in thought.

Her friend knew as soon as she saw Mary's face that something was wrong.

"Is it Michael, has he had an accident?" asked Brigid.

Mary shook her head, unable to speak for a few seconds.

"It's James," she said.

A wave of relief swept over Brigid, just for a moment, then she felt bad.

"What happened, is he not well? Sit down and let me take Catherine."

Brigid placed the child beside her son, Francis. As the two babies lay on the bed kicking their legs into the air, Mary told her about the message from Sunderland.

"What do you make of it?" Brigid asked. "Do you think he is worse than Rose is letting on?"

"I do," said Mary, "She would never have gone behind his back if it wasn't serious. Don't we ourselves know many a poor soul taken by pneumonia?"

Brigid tried to reassure Mary by reminding her how fit her husband was.

"I need to talk this over with Pat and Annie, but if I go to James, would you be willing to help them take care of Catherine?"

"Of course I would. She can even have some of my milk," assured Brigid. "Sure, isn't she taking meal and broth now? I know there will be no talking you out of it, if you make your mind up to go, but please Mary, be sure you are doing the right thing."

When Mary returned home, Annie was back from foraging in the woods but Pat was still at the bog, cutting turf with some of the other men and boys from the village. The old woman was very upset to hear of her nephew's condition.

"I'm sorry I had to break such bad news to you, Annie. I want to ask your advice about something. I already know what Pat will say, but you will understand my reasons better than any man."

Annie took hold of the young woman's hands. "I know what you are thinking, Mary, and if it was my husband lying on a sickbed in a strange land I would be on the first boat over. Does that answer your question?"

Mary smiled, "Pat will go mad, won't he?"

"You leave that old goat to me. I might walk up to the bog and meet him on his way home. Better to break the news about James to him when he is out in the fresh air."

By the time Annie met up with her husband it was quite late and he was nearly home. He was surprised to see her, usually she would be at the house preparing food and keeping the fire going. As he got closer, the smile faded from his tired face.

"Have you been crying?" asked Pat, putting an arm around her shoulder.

Annie nodded and wiped her eyes. "James is sick, he has pneumonia." She gave him the news that had come from England.

They walked along in silence, not a sound being made by their footsteps on the grassy track. Each time a group of men or boys passed by, all the old couple could give was a wave of the hand, too sad to return the usual banter that always accompanied the end of a day at the bog.

"Why were you walking on your own, Pat?" the thought suddenly struck Annie.

Her husband shrugged his shoulders, saying, "I'm an old man now, love. I got tired and had to leave before the others."

Telling him that Mary was planning on going to James, Annie asked what he thought about it.

"What difference would it make how I felt? That young woman is as stubborn as you. Once she has an idea in her head about something there's no changing her mind, is there?" There was more than a hint of annoyance in Pat's voice.

Annie replied, "Now don't be mad at me, but I sold two of my wooden bowls to that woman who . . ."

"YOU WHAT?" roared Pat.

His wife jumped at the sound of it, as did two young men who had just walked past them.

"I could have raised the money for the fare. You can go and get them back, do you hear?" Pat admonished, in a slightly quieter voice.

"All right so, I can do that. Calm down will you? Just don't tell Mary what I did," said Annie sheepishly.

Mary was standing by the fire when the door opened. She saw the worried look on Pat's face. Trying to keep everything as normal as possible she smiled at the elderly couple as she placed some food on the table. "Annie, two of your bowls are missing, did you lend them to someone?"

Pat glared at his wife and slammed the door shut. He walked past Mary and climbed the stairs to his bed. The two women looked at each other for a moment, then Annie confessed to Mary what she had done with her bowls.

"Oh no! There was no need to sell them. I have enough to get me to Liverpool."

Mary was distraught and feeling guilty for being the reason the older woman had parted with such treasured family heirlooms.

"People are more important than things, Mary," said Annie. "Don't mind Pat, his pride is hurt. He feels he's let us down because I had to sell something to raise a bit of money. We have never had to do anything like that in all the years we have been together."

When Annie excused herself to go upstairs to her husband, Mary poured the broth she had made back into the cauldron, having lost her appetite. She picked up her baby to cuddle her but Catherine squirmed and wriggled, as if she knew her mother was about to leave her.

"Don't be cross, little one. Don't you want me to fetch your daddy home? Sure you'll have a great time without your mammy to scold you. Pat and Annie spoil you rotten, don't they?"

As she was tickling her daughter under the chin, Pat appeared at the bottom of the stairs. He sat on the bench beside her, smiling at Catherine.

"So, you are determined to go, are you?" he asked, not taking his eyes off the gurgling baby.

"I am, Pat," she said, continuing to play with the child.

"What if I went instead, Mary? Would that make any difference?"

The young woman placed a hand on the old man's shoulder and looked him in the eye.

"You are the kindest man I know. I can see where James gets his soft heart from, but Catherine and Francis need a man about the place to look after them. Who else but you could do that, with both of their fathers away?"

Annie crept quietly down the stairs, not wanting to interrupt the conversation she knew would be taking place. Hearing the tail end of it, she smiled at how tactfully the young woman spoke. Before she even saw his face, Annie knew that her husband had resigned himself to the fact that Mary was leaving.

Crossing the room to the fireplace, Annie peered into the cauldron and sniffed. "Something smells good," she said.

CHAPTER FOURTEEN

Mary stood on deck, one hand waving, the other in the pocket of her heavy woollen skirt. She was clutching the shells her daughter had picked up from the beach the day before as a present for James. The sight of the little girl waving goodbye almost broke Mary's heart. Pat had hoisted Catherine onto his shoulders so that her mother would see her as the boat moved away.

"Is that your little one with her grandfather?" asked a young woman standing next to Mary.

"It is. She doesn't realize that I won't be back for a long time, her father is sick in England and I'm going over to nurse him."

"What ails him, not the fever, I hope?"

Keeping her eyes glued to the quayside, Mary was afraid to blink in case she lost sight of her family. "He has pneumonia," she said.

A young boy came up to them and dragged the woman to the other side of the deck. Mary was glad to be left alone, to savour the image of Catherine smiling and waving until she became a soft blur in the distance. Just as James had done, she stood looking back at the land until it disappeared from view.

The deck was crowded and noisy, babies crying, children complaining and women shouting at their disgruntled offspring. The men were quiet – too quiet. Mary tried to read the expressions on some of their faces. She imagined what it must have been like for James to stand on deck, surrounded by such chaos, knowing he was a man who preferred solitude. He loved to be out with his uncle in the bay, or on the beach repairing the nets, laying them out over the upturned boats. Everything about her husband's life was the total opposite of what Mary was experiencing at that moment.

She knew it would be even worse in Liverpool, with people arriving from, not just Dundalk, but Dublin, Drogheda, Belfast, and from other countries, too. Mary closed her eyes and tried to block out the sounds, but it didn't work. She kept them shut tight, not wanting to look at the poverty and distress of her fellow passengers, or '*deckers*,' as the crew called them. Not once did Mary consider herself as poor as those around her. Being content with her lot, she felt blessed to have a roof over her head, a good husband, a healthy child and people who cared about her. The lack of money was unfortunate as far as Mary was concerned but her life was rich in other ways. Now and then, someone would ask the young woman a question, or try to make conversation, but her eyes remained closed as she pretended to be asleep.

When the ship docked, there was a rush to disembark. Standing on the quayside,

Mary looked around for a shop or a ticket office, where she might ask for directions and advice about transport to Sunderland. The sound of horses' hooves on the cobblestoned road failed to alert Mary to the fact that a coach was fast approaching. As the crowd parted, the driver saw the young woman and reined in the horses. Mary turned at the last minute, suddenly realizing the danger she was in. It was too late; one of the animals knocked her aside as it came to a halt, sending her flying against a wooden barrel, head first.

As Mary was trying to pick herself up, firm hands grasped her shoulders, steadying the shaken young woman.

"Is she hurt, Alexander?" a well-spoken female voice enquired from within the carriage.

The gentleman who had come to her aid stood back, releasing Mary. There was a large red mark on her temple and some scratches to the side of her face from the rough wood she had landed on.

"Are you about to swoon, my dear?" he asked.

Mary looked up into the eyes of a tall, stocky man in his late thirties.

"I do feel a little strange, sir," she said, "But I will be fine in a minute or two."

She held onto the barrel to steady herself, embarrassed by the stares of the crowd gathering around them.

"Alexander, offer the poor girl a seat in our carriage," the soft voice urged from inside the cab.

The gentleman insisted that Mary sit up beside the driver, at least until they were clear of the crowded docks. Anxious to escape from the onlookers surrounding her, she allowed herself to be steered towards the coach and pulled up onto the seat by a strong pair of hands.

"Driver, watch that she doesn't have a fainting spell and fall off. Stop somewhere less crowded and clear of the docks."

The young lady was upset that her husband had not brought Mary inside the carriage and she berated him for his lack of compassion.

"Emma, you are so sweet and caring, it's what I loved about you from the moment we met," the gentleman spoke tenderly to his wife. "Do you remember what you were doing when your father first brought me to your home?"

"Of course I do, my parents still scold me over it, even though it was so long ago." When her father first introduced Alexander to his family, Emma was cradling a dead robin in her arms, wrapped in a piece of muslin. "I was convinced that if I held the poor thing for long enough and nursed it, that it would recover," she laughed. "I had even kept it in my bed the night before, unbeknownst to my mother."

The memory brought a smile to her face and she patted her husband's hand. Alexander Somerville, as a young man, had been invited to the Biggs' home in London when Emma was a child. His visits became a regular occurrence and over the years, the family grew very fond of him – particularly young Emma. As soon as she was old enough, they married.

"You grew more loving as the years went by. Even now, as a wife and mother, you still have the sweetest nature," Alexander kissed the back of her gloved hand.

"You are becoming quite soft in your old age," Emma was referring to the age gap between them. "But obviously not soft enough to let that young girl ride in the carriage with us." She was no longer smiling.

Alexander also became serious and his wife could hear it in his tone. "That young woman may have been on one of the boats arriving from Ireland. She could have typhus or some other disease. It's not so long ago I was sick with a fever in Dublin and almost died. Do you think I want to risk you catching something like that – and what about our children, are they to be left motherless?"

Emma knew he was right and felt grateful for his concern. There was no need to answer his question, a slight nod of her head was enough to let Alexander know that she understood.

Soon the horses came to a halt and the driver opened the carriage door.

"I hope you haven't been too frightened up there, young lady," Alexander said, looking up at Mary.

"No sir, I have been on top of hay carts much higher than this," Mary hoped she didn't sound too cheeky.

The driver offered a hand to the young woman to help her down, but Alexander stopped him.

"Stay seated for a moment, my dear. Tell me, what is your destination?"

"I am on my way to Sunderland. My husband has pneumonia and I want to be with him."

Alexander questioned Mary about her health and where she had travelled from, then signalled the driver to help her climb down. Asking her to wait while he spoke with his wife, he disappeared back into the carriage.

They both agreed that Mary did not seem to have any sign of illness and they should offer her assistance. Emma's reason being her kind nature and that it was their fault that Mary had been injured. Alexander on the other hand, being a writer and a journalist, was more interested in her story. The door of the carriage opened and a small, gloved hand beckoned Mary to climb inside. Having shut the door, the driver took his seat and once more the horses were on the move.

Mary sat looking at the strange couple, the woman quite a few years younger than her husband. She waited for one of them to say something, but they just kept smiling at her. The silence was becoming awkward so Mary cleared her throat, getting ready to thank them for their kindness. Just as she opened her mouth to speak the young lady asked if she had any children.

"A little girl barely one year old, ma'am. Her name is Catherine."

"Such a lovely name; is she with her father?" enquired Emma.

Mary explained that she had left her daughter with relatives in Ireland. Alexander asked if she would be willing to tell him her story in exchange for some money, explaining that he might use it in his work.

"We are on our way to board a train for Manchester and I would like to buy you a ticket," said Alexander. "From there we can arrange some transport for you to Sunderland. Does this sound agreeable to you?"

Mary did not have to think too long about it. "All you ask in return is my story, is that correct, sir?"

Alexander nodded and assured their young passenger that she would be well rewarded.

When they arrived at the station and had booked their seats, Emma suggested a meal in a nearby hotel. While Mary forced herself to eat slowly and with as much grace as she could muster, Alexander took out a pencil and paper. Emma suggested they finish their meal first, saying it was rude to write at the table and that there was plenty of time before their train arrived.

A short while later, Mary found herself sitting in a sunny conservatory facing Emma and Alexander, a highly polished, mahogany table separating her from the smiling couple. It was laid with a silver teapot and delicate bone china cups and saucers. A waiter soon arrived with a collection of small cakes, neatly arranged on a silver cake stand.

Emma declined the delicacies but Alexander ate three of them. Mary managed one, in spite of being full after, what seemed to her, a very large meal. The sensation of a full stomach was something she had not had for a very long time. Mary wanted to gather up the remaining food to bring with her for the journey and to share with James, but didn't like to appear greedy. Every so often, as she told her story, her gaze would rest briefly on the silver cake stand, but Mary never interrupted her flow of words, conscious of the interest on the faces of the couple in front of her.

When it was time to board their train, Alexander went to settle the account. Emma beckoned to a waiter, who came over with an empty tray to clear the table, and she whispered something to him, pointing to the cakes. Mary watched with disappointment as the remaining food was returned to the kitchen, annoyed with herself for not asking if she could take some with her. Having paid the bill, Alexander signalled to his wife that it was time to go. As the two women walked towards the door the waiter returned carrying a white cotton bundle, tied up with a blue ribbon. He handed it to Mary and Emma thanked him.

"I thought you might like to have them for your journey," said Emma. "You will have to stay overnight in lodgings and if it is late when you arrive there may be nothing left to eat but stale bread. It has happened to me before, so now I travel well prepared."

Mary thanked the young woman for her thoughtfulness and followed the couple across the street onto the station platform. Boarding the train and taking their seats in a beautifully decorated carriage, the couple chatted to Mary about their own children. A lot of what they said went over her head as she watched, with fascination, the world outside pass by. It was Mary's first train journey but she tried to hide that fact by not allowing her excitement to show on her face.

All too soon, the train was steaming into the station in Manchester. Emma brought Mary to a waiting room while Alexander went about some business that needed seeing to. A short while later, he came back with a newspaper and handed it to Mary. She was too embarrassed to let them know she couldn't read.

"Thank you very kindly, sir. I'm not one for reading much myself, but my husband will be delighted. Is this the paper that your stories go into?"

"Yes, it is. I thought you might like something for the journey," responded Alexander. "There is a coach leaving soon for Newcastle with a delivery of goods and some passengers. It will be on its way in about an hour. The driver assures me it will pass through Sunderland. He will be looking out for a young woman of your description holding a newspaper. I expect you are anxious to join your husband, so I took the liberty of arranging the transport for you. I hope you don't mind."

Mary was delighted, as the thought of making her way across the country alone was daunting.

"Thank you so much for all your kindness, both of you. I wish there was some way I could repay it."

"No need to think like that, my dear," said Alexander, "Allowing me to write down your story is payment in full. I may use it in a book I plan on publishing."

Mary was to wait at the station until the coach driver arrived and felt very much alone as she bade farewell to Alexander and Emma. As she watched the couple blend into

102

the crowd, arm in arm, a longing for James swept through her.

"Just one more day. One more day," she whispered to herself.

CHAPTER FIFTEEN

The old man eased his stiff body into an upright position and shuffled to his front door. Opening it, he complained about being dragged from his chair. Squinting against the shaft of sunlight washing over him, it took a few seconds before he realized what the pretty young woman who stood on his doorstep was saying.

"I'm sorry, dearie, which of the McGrothers did you say you were looking for? There's a few of them in this street."

Mary took a breath and spoke much slower, asking for the second time about Owen and Rose. Her eyes followed the direction of a crooked, arthritic finger pointing to a door across the street. Thanking him, she ran to the other side and knocked. Straightening the creases from her skirt and checking her hair was still in place, Mary waited for the door to open.

"Who is it?" a small voice called out.

"Is that wee Jamie I hear? It's your Auntie Mary. Uncle James's wife, all the way from Ireland."

The door slowly opened and a small face appeared.

"Do you remember me? I used to spin you around until we were both giddy." Mary was impatient to see her husband but didn't want to alarm the child by rushing into the house.

"Is James in there with you?" she asked.

The young boy nodded and opened the door wide, a puzzled expression on his face. As Mary stepped inside, James's sister Maggie came down the stairs carrying a wash bowl and cloth. She almost tripped on the last step at the sight of who was standing in the parlour. Mary rushed over to her, laughing and crying at the same time. The two women embraced, then Maggie stood back, pointing to a chair.

"Sit down, just for a minute or two. I know you must be anxious to see James but there's something you should be prepared for."

"I'm listening, go on," implored Mary, her heart pounding with a mix of anxiety and excitement.

"The pneumonia took a lot out of James, we nearly lost him. With nourishing broth and plenty of rest he is making a good recovery. Rose has been a great help, asking the doctors at the infirmary where she works how best to look after him."

"Can I see him, please? I have come such a long way. I promise not to wake him if he is asleep, I just want to be near him." Mary was pleading.

Maggie felt sorry for her sister-in-law. James was no longer the smiling young man that melted the hearts of his older siblings. His eyes had become dull and sad, giving the impression that he wasn't quite there; even though he responded to questions and took his food. A simple "yes" or "no" was all any of the family could get out of him as he lay in bed, turning his back to them most of the time.

"He's not in any danger now from the pneumonia," Maggie continued. "The doctor said he is suffering from melancholia because of his illness. The shortage of food for the past year has weakened him, making recovery slower. Rose told me she sent for you, but the rest of the family don't know. James's brothers would not go against his wishes, you know what men are like." Maggie rolled her eyes and pinched her little nephew on the cheek. "You will grow up to be just as stubborn, my young man," she said to the smiling child.

"Are you telling me James won't want to see me?" cried Mary.

Maggie took the young woman's hand and held it in both of hers. "James wants to see you with all his heart. It is *you* seeing *him* that bothers him. Men are proud, Mary – James feels he has let his family down. He told Owen he would rather die than go on being a burden to them. Rose overheard it and that was when she decided to get a message to you."

Maggie stood, pulling Mary up with her.

"Now, do you think you are ready to see that young husband of yours?" she asked.

Taking a deep breath, Mary composed herself and nodded, ready to deal with whatever way her husband chose to greet her. She would be delighted if he was happy to see her, but having been warned of his frame of mind, she would not let it upset her if he was angry – or worse still, ignored her completely. Mary felt as if she were climbing a mountain with every step on the stairs that took her nearer to James. Outside the bedroom door she paused nervously, her hand raised in a tight fist, ready to knock.

CHAPTER SIXTEEN

A gentle tap on the door failed to elicit a response from the young man who lay facing the wall, a grey woollen blanket pulled over his shoulder. Mary slowly pushed open the door and crept into the darkened room. The only sound was the high pitched squeals of children playing in the street outside, filtering through the closed window. Mary had the best of intentions when she began to climb the stairs. If she found James sleeping, she was determined to wait until he woke up, to be patient and let him have his rest. All her resolve melted upon entering the room. The frame that lay under the cover was a shrunken version of the man who had kissed her goodbye on the quayside in Dundalk.

"James, are you awake, do you need anything?" whispered Mary, standing just inside the door.

There was a slight movement of the blanket as he answered and the emptiness in his voice tore into her heart.

"No thank you, Maggie," James thought that his sister had come back up the stairs.

Mary tip toed across the room and sat on the edge of the bed. She gently stroked the back of his head, curling his hair around her finger out of habit. The young man's body stiffened and Mary waited for an angry outburst.

James was unable to speak, even though he knew from the touch who it was behind him. He did not want his wife to see him in such a state. For the first time in weeks he felt emotion stirring, as gentle hands caressed his shoulders. Soft fingers wove through his hair, making his scalp tingle. Slowly turning around, his eyes closed, James reached up searching for the face he knew was above him. His palm cradled a tear stained cheek then curved around a slender neck. The familiar touch broke through the wall of sadness that James had built around himself and he drew Mary towards him, releasing his love with a gentle kiss.

Silently, they lay clinging to each other for a long time, until voices and laughter from below alerted them to the fact that Rose was home. Mary sat up, fixing her hair back into place, and wiped her tears away.

"Close your eyes and hold out your hand, I have something for you, from Catherine – a present she chose all by herself."

Mary reached into her pocket. James did as she said and felt some cold, small objects being placed in his upturned palm.

"Smell them," whispered Mary.

His eyes still closed, James brought his hand up to his nose and immediately an image of the sea flashed through his mind. Tears streamed down his face as he clutched the shells in his fist, holding them close to his heart.

"Mary, go on down to Rose, she will be anxious to see you. Leave me on my own for a little while to gather myself together."

"You're not mad at me, are you, or at Rose for sending for me?" she asked.

James smiled and shook his head. "So that's how you found out," he said. "No, I'm not mad at anyone. Not even at myself anymore."

Mary kissed him before leaving the room. James felt drained, but it wasn't the empty feeling he had before. It was a pleasant tiredness. He struggled out of bed, determined to join his family for supper, something he had not been able to do since his arrival. The laughter of his brother Owen, as he lifted Mary to swing her around the parlour, drifted up the stairs to James. The sound of it made him smile as he took his first shaky step, back into his life.

CHAPTER SEVENTEEN

Owen and Rose's parlour was filled to the brim with relatives. Their children had called to the various houses on the street announcing Mary's arrival. By the time James rounded the bend in the stairs, most of the family had gathered, including some neighbours who were caught up in the excitement of it all. There was an abrupt silence as soon as James made an appearance and Owen ran over towards him as he was about to collapse on the last step. Peter, another of his brothers, gave a hand and between them they half carried the young man to a chair by the fireside. Rose wrapped a blanket around his knees and the laughter and well-wishing started up again. Everyone was throwing questions at Mary and she had to ask them to take it in turns so she could hear them clearly. The evening was spent listening to news from home and the events of Mary's trip over.

When Rose noticed that James was looking quite drained she whispered into her husband's ear. Owen stood up and clapped his hands together.

"Well now, I think we should let the young couple spend a bit of time together, and all you children should get to your beds before it's time to get up," he said, herding his own young ones towards the stairs.

One by one, the visitors shook hands with James and Mary as they left the house and when the last one was gone Rose let out a sigh of relief.

"I think myself that one or two from the next street hid themselves amongst us. What do you say, Owen?" her husband had just come down the stairs.

"I daresay they did, sure doesn't the same thing happen every time we have a bit of a céilidh? The sound of Peter's fiddle attracts them like bees to honey." Owen put an arm around his wife's shoulder and smiled over at the young couple, "I've been waiting a long time to have the both of ye together under my roof. You're a sight for sore eyes, Mary, love."

"I have something to give you but I couldn't take it out with the crowd that was here, there wouldn't have been enough to go round." Mary handed Rose the white cloth bag, tied with a blue ribbon. "I brought these cakes from Liverpool for the children. They might be a wee bit stale but I'm sure they won't mind."

The two women embraced and Rose, for the tenth time that evening, told Mary how happy she was to have her with them.

Owen offered to help his brother back to bed, but James said he wanted to stay by the fire with Mary for a while.

"I've spent long enough in that bed, it's good to be out of it," he said.

"We'll go on up and leave you two alone, so. The children have carried their mattresses into our room, so you both have a bit of privacy," Rose said.

"I'm sure you will have a lot of catching up to do," Owen winked at James.

Rose slapped him on the back and pulled him by the hand towards the stairs, laughing.

As James stared into the fire, Mary pulled a chair next to his and held his hand. He wrapped part of his blanket around her knees and they sat together, neither one feeling the need to speak – she with her head resting on his shoulder and he kissing her hair.

Their intimate silence was broken by a light tap on the window. A young man's face was pressed against the glass and Mary ran to open the door. The cool, night air carried in with it the smell of alcohol, as Michael stepped inside. He looked very sheepish as Mary sniffed, scolded and hugged him.

"Honestly, it's only the odd time I go for a drink. I swear to you, Mary."

The young woman stood, hands on her hips, looking from one man to the other. "What are ye like, the pair of ye? One drowns in his sorrow while the other drowns in his drink. I think I got here just in time."

"I was just in the door when Maggie sent me over to look in the window, she said someone might still be up. She told me you

113

had arrived earlier, Mary. I got such a shock when I saw himself sitting there at the fireside. What magic did you use to get him out of his bed, we have all tried to coax him downstairs, but nothing worked?" Michael patted James's back.

The young couple smiled at each other. James reached into his jacket and held out his hand to Michael.

"It was a handful of shells that did it, a present from Catherine. Although, seeing Mary helped a bit, too."

Mary pulled her chair aside for Michael to sit down. She lowered herself gently onto James's knee, his arm automatically curling around her small waist. It gave him the feeling of being back home, in his aunt and uncle's house. Michael smiled wistfully at the two of them and James knew how much he was missing Brigid, although he would never admit it.

"How is my wee family keeping back home, Mary?"

"Brigid and Francis are both very well, Pat and Annie are taking good care of them, and our little Catherine, too."

Michael stared into the red glow of the slack covered coals. "Strange," he said, "I don't think we ever had a coal fire in our house, I'm sure I never sat at one until I came to England, did you, James?"

The young couple exchanged puzzled glances.

"No, I don't think I did, it was always turf fires at home. Why do you ask?" replied James.

After a minute of silence there was a deep sigh from Michael as he turned to face them, "Do you think my Brigid would like it here, Mary?"

CHAPTER EIGHTEEN

The following morning, James watched Mary as she tidied around the parlour. He lifted Jamie, his young nephew, up onto his lap so he could reach the table with more ease and eat from his bowl, without dribbling the food all over his clothes. Those small, familiar actions served to anchor him in the present. They reminded James he had a part to play in other people's lives and a family that needed him and his resolve to get his health back grew stronger.

"Maggie is delighted to have a day to herself," said Mary, "And young Jamie doesn't seem to be missing her too much, yet."

"Catherine must be missing you though. Maybe you shouldn't stay too long, one of us needs to be with her." James didn't want her to go, but felt the need to say it, hating to see her torn between her husband and her daughter.

"James McGrother, I did not come all the way over here to go back without you. We are going home together, never mind the work. We can manage, like we always have."

James was quiet for a moment, gathering his thoughts. If he returned with Mary, his trip would have been a waste of time. At least there was work in England for him. He just needed to save enough money to see them through to the next harvest, three months away.

"Do you think Brigid will move over here with Francis, to be with Michael?" Mary asked, her question breaking into his thoughts.

James noticed that his nephew had finished his breakfast and sat him down on the bench beside him before answering.

"I think she will, Mary. Are you thinking of moving here yourself?"

"No, I could never live here, not unless it meant a better life for Catherine, which I doubt."

James stood and stretched his legs, relieved at what his wife had said. He could never leave Ireland for good, but a few months away wouldn't do him any harm. Having been so sick both in health and spirit, James knew he would never allow those feelings to suffocate him again. As long as he was fit, there was no reason for him to go back with Mary. He would talk her into going home to Catherine and letting him get on with what he had set out to do in the first place.

"Let's take young Jamie for a walk, the fresh air will do us all some good," he said.

CHAPTER NINETEEN

Mary reluctantly agreed to return home before the week was out, but only because James promised that he would be careful with his health and would stay no longer than three months. Owen had secured him a job at the forge where he worked, that way, an eye could be kept on his younger brother. The heat of the place would be better than being outdoors shovelling soil or breaking stone in wet weather, as Michael was doing.

"The pay is not so good, James, but the work will be a lot more manageable for you after the illness you've just come through."

"Thank you, Owen. I'll do any job, as long as I can save a bit of money to send home, and of course pay my way here, too, Rose." James did not want to be a burden on them.

His sister-in-law smiled and looked across the room at her husband. Owen smiled back, remembering the conversation they had been having that morning, before leaving the house. Owen had confessed to Rose that his boss at the forge would take James on, if he would take a cut in his wages. He had agreed without discussing it with her and at first Rose had been annoyed.

"Oh, it's done now, so let's not fuss about it anymore," she had said, "Anyway, if I know James, he will insist on paying for his keep, so we won't be any worse off than we are now."

"Make sure you don't let it slip, or tell anyone. He would never forgive me if he found out," Owen had replied.

The night before Mary's departure, Michael called to see her. He was just home from work and Rose invited him to stay for dinner.

"I've just had some at Maggie's, thanks," he said.

"Well I'm sure you can fit another wee bit in, couldn't you?" Rose was already filling up a bowl for him.

Michael turned to Mary and said, "See how I can get two suppers in one day here. Sure why would I want to go back to Ireland, where I am lucky some days to get any? Would you not consider moving over, Mary? At least for a year."

As she opened her mouth to answer, James took hold of her hand and squeezed it. She took a spoonful of food instead, grateful for being rescued from an argument that would have developed around the table, had she spoken her mind. She shook her head and smiled at Michael. Everyone, except James and Mary, felt they had made a fresh start by leaving their homeland. They didn't need to be reminded of their heritage, their ancestors, or their roots. They were more concerned about the future, for themselves and their children.

The atmosphere that evening remained light and pleasant, in spite of the fact that a member of the family was soon to leave. Michael gave Mary some money to bring home to Brigid. There was enough to clear any debts she might have and pay her passage over. He would meet her in Liverpool off the same ship that Mary had arrived on.

"Do you need money yourself?" he asked.

"Mary earned herself a nice little sum selling her story to a newspaper man on the way over. The laugh of it is, my wife has earned more than I have in this country so far," teased James.

"Why James McGrother, I do believe you are jealous," exclaimed Mary. "Maybe it is me should stay and you go home to Catherine."

Michael went very quiet and pulled a newspaper from the inside pocket of his jacket. Mary recognized it as being similar to the one she had been given by the gentleman who helped her make her way to Sunderland. James was the only one in the family who could read and Michael handed him the paper.

"One of the men I work with said there was something in here about a young Irish woman who was travelling across England to meet up with her sick husband. He said he was finished reading it and that I could take it with me. I never thought for a minute it could be you, Mary, I was going to make a jest of it," said Michael.

A hush fell across the room as James read what Alexander Somerville had written.

Apparently, the article was one of an ongoing series that had been published about the conditions in Ireland due to two years of potato blight, evictions and a great hunger throughout the land.

Michael was first to break the silence.

"Is that what you want to go home to? James, talk some sense into your wife, make her see how bad it really is there, and it can only get worse. I'm sorry, Mary, I have to go. I am only going to upset you if I stay."

He embraced her and left, apologizing once more for his outburst. Poor Mary felt the eyes of everyone in the room on her. James took hold of his wife's hand and looked around at his family.

"It's me that wants to stay at home, you all know how I feel about moving away. Mary would settle here with Catherine if it was what I wanted, she told me so yesterday. Besides, Pat and Annie need us, they are like parents to us and are the last of that generation left in our family."

Nobody spoke for a minute until Owen stood up and announced he was going to get Peter to come up with his fiddle.

"Let's give Mary an Irish send off," he said, telling his children to gather the relatives and neighbours together.

Mary's cheeks were damp with tears as James held her close. She could hear the steady beat of his heart and closed her eyes, memorizing it's comforting sound for those lonely nights ahead, when she would lie awake missing him.

CHAPTER TWENTY

Clapping her hands and stamping her feet, just like the adults, young Catherine was the image of her mother. Pat lifted her up and swung her around the parlour. Annie held Francis in her arms as she danced among the neighbours, the two children loving the fact that they were now eye to eye with the adults around them. Brigid and Mary sat down, out of breath.

"The McGrothers know how to throw a party, that's for sure," said Mary, "This is the second one I've been to in a week."

Brigid laughed and hugged her friend, "Oh Mary, I wish you were coming, too. I will miss you so much."

The two young women were dragged back up onto the floor, cutting short their conversation. Mary was glad of the interruption, there had been too many goodbyes for her lately. It was good to see so many happy faces and hear the children laughing, in spite of the harsh times most of them struggled with. She did not want to think about the next day, when she would have to watch another friend take the boat.

The following morning, Mary and Catherine stood on the quayside, waving. She knew what it felt like to be in Brigid's shoes at that moment. The prospect of being reunited with her husband would ease the pain of leaving her home and friends behind.

However, Brigid was going for good. Mary knew by the words Michael had spoken that he would never return. He had bitterness in his heart and she feared he might even take his wife and child as far away as America. Then she would never see them again.

Pat laid his arm gently on Mary's shoulder. He held Catherine in his other arm as she laughed and waved at Francis, up on deck.

"Smile for your friend, Mary. Don't let her last image of your pretty face be one of sadness. There's plenty of time for that when we go home," he counselled.

It was as if he could read her thoughts.

"I know, Pat. Sure look at the state of her – she's crying enough for both of us."

They stayed watching the steam ship until it was so far out that the people on board couldn't be seen any more. The two mile walk back home was a quiet one, Catherine's baby-talk the only thing breaking their silence.

Annie was stirring the pot over the fire when they walked through the door. She swept her little grandniece into her arms and kissed her soft hair.

"Why the long face, Mary? Sure when times are better you can always visit them in England – and won't they be home at some stage themselves, to see the family?" Annie was trying to comfort Mary.

The young woman looked sadly at Pat and he shrugged his shoulders. He knew what she was thinking. Mary excused herself and ran up the stairs, leaving Catherine with Annie.

"Have I upset her by what I said, Pat, I didn't mean to?"

"No, Annie, she just needs some time alone. That felt very much like a final farewell on the quayside this morning."

"Not at all, it's only a short journey across the water, young people are always coming and going between here and Liverpool," Annie asserted as she scooped up Catherine to give her a cuddle, "Isn't that so, little woman?"

Pat looked at the smile on his wife's face and thought better of putting any sad thoughts into her head. He knew Michael had a lot of anger bottled up over the conditions in Ireland and being in England wasn't going to melt it away, it could very well make it worse.

"You're right, love, sure we have plenty of room here for them when they visit. Maybe we can take a trip over ourselves sometime."

Annie stopped playing with Catherine and looked at her husband. "Now you *are* talking nonsense, Pat McGrother. Sure you can't even go the two miles to Dundalk without feeling homesick, never mind a trip to England."

As Mary lay upstairs, her eyes red and swollen from crying, the laughter of her family in the parlour below, swept like a gentle wave into the bedroom. She sat up, wiped her face and took a deep breath. Her life was good, there were people much worse off than she was. Catherine would love a walk on the beach and Annie might join them. Maybe they would find that extra special shell they always looked for – or maybe they wouldn't. The time spent together was reward enough for Mary.

CHAPTER TWENTY-ONE

"Are you alright?" asked Michael, concerned at the fit of coughing his friend was having. James nodded, took a deep breath and began another bout.

"Sorry, Michael, I will have to go outside for some fresh air."

"I don't know about it being fresh, it's a wonder we're not all choking, living here," said Michael, who had been on edge all evening.

James felt better in the cool night air. It was very seldom he accompanied his friend, or even his brothers, on their trips to the local public houses. He wasn't much of a drinker and hated to put his hard earned money into other people's pockets. Most of his wages got sent home to Mary.

"Let's walk back home, James, there's something I need to tell you."

The two friends were silent as they walked along the busy streets, ignoring the begging children, who should have been in bed, and the women who came up to them touting for business.

"We're not interested, go home to your parents," said Michael as he and James pried the arms of two young women from around their necks.

"Hah! Our mother is out here with us. We can go get her if it's an older woman that interests you," one of them spat back as they ran off laughing.

"They didn't look more than fifteen," Michael was visibly upset. "This is not the place I want to bring up my children. Brigid and myself have talked it over and come to a decision."

"She's going back to Ireland, I knew it. We can make a go of it there, Michael, things will get better and we can help each other out."

Michael looked at his friend's beaming face. He hadn't seen him smile like that since Mary's visit, and he tried to find the right words for what he had to say.

"No James. There's nothing back there for us either. We are leaving for America as soon as we have enough money saved. You know I've always loved working the land. While I'm still young enough and have the strength and courage to do it, I want to have a go at that homesteading we're always hearing about. Think of it James, owning your own land. No landlord or his agent telling you what to plant, taking all your harvest as rent. Even worse, evicting you or paying you to emigrate, so as to pull down your home and run sheep or cattle across the land." Michael stopped to take a breath. "Come with us, James."

"Michael, you know I'm not a farmer. I'm a fisherman, I couldn't survive being stuck in the middle of a vast foreign land. You are a fisherman, too. How can you even think of going?"

James knew by the look on his friend's face that it was useless to try and talk Michael out of his decision.

"My father is a fisherman, but I always wanted to be a farmer. Your father worked as a farm hand, James, but *I* am going to *own* the land I work."

The mention of James's father working the land brought back a memory. It was one of the few he had of a time before his parents died and although he would only have been about four years old, the image was crystal clear in his head. He was sitting on his father's shoulders, listening to him name the different wild plants and flowers they came across on their walk along the hedgerows. No matter what James pointed to, his father could identify it, having a great love of nature. James knew that if his father was in his shoes at that moment, he would be off with Michael in a heartbeat.

"I can see you are determined to go, so I wish you well, Michael. You will be sorely missed, Brigid and Francis, too."

Michael decided to give it one more try to persuade James about going with them.

"How long has your uncle Pat been a fisherman?"

"Most of his life, as you well know," said James.

"And he still doesn't own his own boat, does he?" Michael felt bad saying it, but he wanted to make a point.

James could see where the conversation was going. "Pat is not ambitious, Michael. He's happy enough to be part of a crew. Himself and Annie manage fine, in spite of the hunger that has a grip on Ireland."

"Do you honestly think that you will ever have your own boat, James?"

Feeling the need to defend both himself and his uncle, James squared his shoulders and thumped his chest with a clenched fist.

"I have dreams too, Michael, just like you, only mine are of home and the sea. If I want my own boat, then I will get one."

The two friends stood facing each other, their stance rigid and unyielding.

"How soon do you think you'll be going, then?" asked James, breaking the tension between them.

"This time Brigid won't let me go without herself and Francis. I wouldn't want them making that crossing on their own anyway, so we agreed to go a month from now. We have enough saved for passage but we need a bit to spare until I get some work. Remember how your cousin Bernard sent word home that he had land needing labourers if anyone wanted to join him over there?"

James nodded, his heart feeling like a lump of lead in his chest.

130

"Well, I hope to join him and when the time is right, stake my own claim."

Michael's eyes were bright as he shared with James the plans that himself and Brigid had talked over, night after night, ever since she arrived. However, his enthusiasm was lost on his friend.

"I knew you two were thinking on something important. Why didn't you tell me sooner?" asked James.

"I didn't want you trying to talk me out of it. When Brigid got here and I told her, she was as excited as I am about it. With her on my side, I knew I could follow through on my goal."

"I understand, Michael. I would have tried to change your mind at first, but I can see how you come to life just talking about America. There are great opportunities there for the right people, but I am not one of them. You and Brigid will achieve whatever you set out to do, I know you will, and you have my best wishes going with you."

James held out his hand and as Michael took it the two friends embraced, an exchange of unspoken love, and sadness, passing between them.

CHAPTER TWENTY-TWO

As Pat approached his cottage he heard a strange sound coming from behind a hedge that separated the garden from the surrounding field. He stopped and listened, thinking he must have imagined it. Then it started again and he knew what it was he was listening to. Dropping his share of the catch from a good night's fishing, Pat ran inside and called out to Annie to come downstairs.

"You were right about Mary; I heard her retching in the field, behind the hedge. Go on out to her Annie and tell her we know what ails her."

Throwing a shawl around her shoulders, Annie stepped outside and heard a soft moan to her left. The air was heavy with the soapy smell of elderflowers opening their petals to the early morning sun. As she got nearer to the hedge, another familiar smell reached her nostrils.

"Mary, come on out of the field, I know why you are in there hiding."

A pale and worried young woman stepped sheepishly out from behind the hedge.

"Oh, Annie, what am I going to do? What will James say? I don't want him to find out, not till he gets back."

The older woman laughed and took hold of Mary's hand. She had suspected a pregnancy some weeks before and said as much to Pat. They had decided to let Mary tell them in her own good time.

"You poor wee mite! Sure James will be delighted with the news. Maybe he will have a son this time."

"Annie, you never look on the bad side of anything, do you? It means another mouth to feed. If James finds out, he may not come home at the end of next month. He will feel obliged to stay in England to earn more money."

"Well now, there's not a lot you can do about the baby, but if you don't want James to find out – then don't tell anyone. Besides yourself, me and Pat are the only ones that know and our lips are sealed. Now come on inside and have some tea to settle your stomach," Annie pulled Mary along behind her.

Pat was bouncing Catherine on his knee when the two women entered the cottage. Annie related to her husband Mary's wish, that James remain ignorant of the situation until his return. She said they should keep the news to themselves for the time being, not telling anyone in the village.

"You won't show for a good while yet, Mary," said Annie, "By then, James will be back and it won't matter who knows. What do you say, Pat?"

"I don't know what you are talking about and that's the way we will leave it. I'm not going to have my nephew accuse me of conspiring with you two, getting him home under false pretence. Now, if you will excuse me, I am going into the field to check my snares – maybe when I come back my good wife will have made me some breakfast."

As Pat reached for the cap he had placed on a hook inside the door, Catherine went to run after him, but Mary held her back. When she was sure her husband was out of earshot, Annie turned to Mary.

"Men and their pride. Don't worry about Pat, he means it when he says he won't say a word. My advice to you, young woman, is to act surprised when James gets back and notices your swollen belly. You can blame the money he sent home and the food it bought for your weight gain. Why, I think I've put on a pound or two myself."

Mary laughed as Annie placed both hands over her flat stomach and puffed out her cheeks.

Early next morning, Mary woke up to the familiar watery feeling in her mouth. She thought if she could just lie still and flat, she might not throw up last night's meagre supper. Pat and Annie were asleep upstairs and Catherine was snuggled up next to her. Mary slowly turned on her side to look at her daughter. Her soft hair was damp with sweat from the body heat they had built up between them.

"There's three of us now," Mary thought as she laid a hand gently on her stomach.

The bile started to rise and knowing she was going to be sick, Mary eased herself off the bed, being careful not to rouse Catherine. The door creaked as it was slowly opened, but not loud enough to disturb the sleeping household. This time Mary didn't make it as far as the hedge, but threw up at the rear of the cottage. Feeling better, although shaky on her feet, she walked back inside the house and gasped at the sight that met her eyes.

A strange, ragged man had Catherine sitting on his knee. She was wide awake and looking up at him, smiling.

"Who are you, what are you doing with my child on your lap?"

Mary was paralyzed with fear for her daughter. Her eyes were drawn to a knife he held in his hand behind the little girl's back. Mary recognized it as Pat's, the one he used for gutting fish.

"I'm sorry to frighten you like this, missus. I won't harm the child. Can you see how desperate I am?"

He looked about fifty, but starvation had that effect on people and Mary guessed he was nearer to thirty. She listened for any sign of a creak from the floor boards upstairs, but it was very early in the morning. As Pat had not been fishing the night before, there was no reason for anyone to be awake. Mary decided that it was probably a good thing he was still asleep. Another person appearing might panic the stranger, who was still holding on to Catherine.

"What is it you want? We have no money in the house and nothing left to sell," said Mary.

"Food, that's all I want. Just give me some food and I'll be on my way."

"Can I put my little one back into her bed, first, she's getting cold?"

The man looked at the small child on his lap and his face softened.

"Fetch a shawl to wrap around her, she's fine where she is," he said.

Mary lifted a blanket from the bed and wrapped it around Catherine. She thought about grabbing her daughter and running outside, but the sight of the knife reminded her of the danger they were in. She had seen the mildest of people driven to madness with hunger.

"You're not from around here, I can't place your accent. Have you travelled far?" Mary was trying to keep as calm as possible.

"No more talking, please – just give me some food and let me leave you in peace."

Catherine began to cry, the change in tone of the man's voice frightening her. He tried to keep a firm grip but in the struggle to get away from him, she slipped out from under the blanket and landed on the floor. Mary scooped her up and turned towards the door, but as she reached the threshold she heard the sound of a chair falling over and a loud thud. When she looked back, the man had passed out on the floor, the chair overturned beside him. The knife was lying six inches away from his outstretched hand.

Pat and Annie were still asleep upstairs, and Mary knew she had to get that knife before the stranger came round. Wrapping the blanket tightly around Catherine's tiny frame, she placed her at the gate, far enough away from the house but still visible from inside the parlour.

"Stay there and hold this blanket around you. I am going to get your auntie Annie to come for a walk with us. Don't move, Catherine, be a good girl."

Mary could see the badly worn soles of the man's boots, a hole in the centre of each of them. His feet didn't move and the knife was still on the floor. She ran passed him and as she bent down, her fingers about to curl around the wooden handle, a bony hand grabbed hold of her ankle.

CHAPTER TWENTY-THREE

A loud scream woke Pat and Annie, their eyes shooting open at the same time. They were on their feet in an instant, a fast move for a couple in their seventies. Pat, being first to reach the bottom of the stairs, was horrified to see Mary sitting on the floor, stabbing a knife into the air at an emaciated man.

"Mary, give me the knife, love. Here, let me help you up." Pat was at her side, pulling her back from the stranger, who had released his grip on her ankle but was still lying on the floor. "What are you doing in my house, frightening my family?" he asked.

There was a low moan and then a sob. Annie stood at the door with Catherine in her arms. Handing the knife back to Mary, Pat told her to stand outside with Annie. The young woman protested that he might be in danger, suggesting they all go outside.

"Mary, look at the poor wretch," said Pat. "He can't even lift himself up off the floor. Go on outside with Annie and let me have a quiet word with him. Give the man a bit of dignity, girl."

"Pat, he had a knife in his hand and Catherine on his knee, he doesn't deserve to be treated with respect. A real man would never threaten a child."

The sobs got louder and everyone turned to look at the man who had managed to raise himself up on one elbow, his body shaking as he cried. Annie pulled the young woman out of the house.

"Come on now, Mary, this is not something you want your child to see or hear," she said.

Pat held out a hand to the stranger and helped him to stand. Picking up the overturned chair, he gestured towards it and the man slumped wearily into the seat.

"Are you going to tell me what this is all about? You don't strike me as someone who would harm a child," said Pat.

"I wouldn't harm a fly and that's the truth, mister. I'm as weak as a kitten, so I won't be a threat to you or your family. I would be very grateful for a little food to bring back to my children. I promise not to bother you again, we are just passing through."

Pat, held out his hand and introduced himself, "And what's your name, friend?" he asked.

"Thomas Gallagher. I'm sorry for acting like a madman. I don't know what came over me. I saw the door open and came inside hoping to find a loaf of bread or something I could grab quickly and run with, before anyone spotted me. I had your knife in my hand because I was going to steal it. It might have bought us a meal. Then your little granddaughter came over to me and hugged my leg. I lifted her up but I was so weak, I had to sit down on the chair. That was when her mother came in and saw me."

"You said you needed food for your children, where are they?" asked Pat.

"Down the road a bit, just before the bend. We slept in the ditch last night. We have been walking for weeks, on our way to Dundalk. I heard that the steamships take on free passengers as ballast whenever they don't have a full cargo on board. I'm hoping to get to Liverpool, I have cousins there."

"Is your wife with you?" asked Pat.

The man hung his head for a moment before answering.

"No, she died two weeks ago, from the fever. We had to go into the workhouse in Carlow, when our food and money ran out. Our family was separated. Me and my eldest boy were put in with the men and my wife and three little ones were in the women's quarters. They made me sign away the lease I had on my land before they would let us in. At least in there, we were guaranteed some food every day, but people were dropping like flies, of the fever. Me and my son were given work to do but when my wife got sick there was no one to mind our little ones. She was taken to the fever shed and I was only allowed visit her once," the man's voice broke and Pat gave him some water. "My wife begged me to take the children to England, to our relatives. I promised her that I would but she died before I had a chance to speak with her again. Five people were buried with her, in a common grave, behind the workhouse. I took my children and left straight after the priest's blessing on the grave. We walked out of the county that five generations of my family have lived in – and I never once looked back."

Pat called Annie and Mary into the cottage, repeating what he had just been told. He asked them to go up to the bend in the road and fetch Thomas's children. Catherine, who had fallen asleep in her mother's arms, was placed on the bed.

"Wake up the fire, Pat. We can make some meal cakes and there's broth from yesterday still in the pot," Annie shouted back as she followed Mary through the door.

In less than five minutes, the two women were at the spot where Thomas's children lay sleeping. The eldest boy was no more than twelve years old and had his arms around two little girls. The youngest, a little boy, was lying face down on top of his older brother, a tattered blanket draped across them as they huddled together to keep warm. Mary cried out when she saw them and the older boy woke up, startled. He tried to get up but fell back onto the ground, the weight of his siblings holding him down. A loud cry from the youngest child woke the others and within seconds three of the children were sobbing, not from fright, but from the hunger

141

that had been gnawing at their stomachs for days.

Annie explained to them that their father was at her house and a meal would be waiting for them there. She picked up the smallest girl and was surprised at how light she was.

"Oh Mary, she doesn't weigh much more than our Catherine, poor wee mite. Can you manage to carry your brother, it's only a five minute walk?" she asked the older boy.

Picking up the other little girl, Mary walked silently behind Annie, thinking on the morning's events. She was no longer mad at Thomas Gallagher, especially after seeing the state that his children were in. He must have been giving them every scrap of food he could find, as he was in worse condition than they were.

Thomas held his arms out to his children as they entered the cottage and the three youngest ran to him. Looking at the man she had wanted to hurt less than half an hour before, with his long thin arms wrapped around his family, Mary was flooded with guilt. She beckoned to the older boy, who was standing just inside the door, cap in hand. Patting a spot on the bench at the table, she smiled at the youngster.

"I can see your parents have brought you up well, young man, taking your cap off like that when you enter a house," Mary said. "It's a fine thing to be able to mind your manners when your belly is crying out for food."

"Indeed it is," said Annie as she poured warm broth into the four wooden bowls and a small clay pot that Pat had placed on the table. The two little girls were seated in an instant, draining the bowls before their father had taken his first mouthful.

"I'm afraid the same cannot be said about your sisters' manners, can it, Tom?" Thomas smiled at his son.

"What are the girls' names?" asked Mary.

"Maggie and Minnie," said Thomas.

"My real name is Mary, but everyone calls me Minnie on account of that being mammy's name too," piped up the younger girl.

"Well now, I'm another Mary, so how about we still call you Minnie so we don't get mixed up?"

The little girl nodded a head full of matted hair.

"And who are you, little man?" asked Annie, lifting the child from his father's lap and placing him on her own.

"Patrick," he shouted, "Not Paddy, Patrick."

Everyone laughed at the loud voice booming out of such a tiny body.

"That's what his mother always said when anyone called him Paddy, in those exact words, too. He's known as Not-Paddy-Patrick, in our family," said Thomas.

"That makes two Patricks in the house as well as two Marys, but you can call *him* Pat," Annie pointed to her husband.

Pat held out his hand so that young Patrick could shake it.

After the meal, Mary suggested herself and Annie take the children to the beach, while the men talked. Tom hung back, watching his younger siblings take hold of each other's hands as they followed the women through the door. Mary looked behind and saw an old man's expression on a young boy's face. She thought to herself how sad it was that his childhood was gone, at twelve years of age. Time spent on the beach, running in and out of the water, looking for shells and sifting the sand through his toes would be far better for him, than listening to the trials and tribulations of the country the men would be discussing.

"Sometimes we find lots of driftwood on the beach. It burns hotter than turf and we could do with a strong pair of arms to help carry it back, Tom," said Mary.

The boy looked at his father, who nodded his head in reply. With a smile on his face, Tom picked up his little brother and sat him on his shoulders, energized by the breakfast he had received.

CHAPTER TWENTY-FOUR

James looked around his brother's parlour. Another farewell party was being held, this time for his best friend. He knew he would probably never see him again. Michael saw the sadness on James's face and looked away. Continuing to dance with Brigid, he held his son in his arms. When the music stopped, he caught James's eye and pointed towards the door and the two men went outside to talk.

"What if one of them Indians shoots an arrow through you, or Brigid for that matter," James asked.

"I shall make friends with them as soon as I get there. Anyway, we will have to earn more money when we get to New York and that means staying there for at least a year, I reckon. My cousin has a room he said we can use in return for Brigid's cooking and housekeeping skills. There's four other Irishmen sharing the house with him and they all miss their mother's cooking. I think my poor wife is going to be more exhausted than me by the end of each week."

"How can you make such a jest of it, Michael? What if you or Brigid cannot bear it over there?"

"Then we come home – as simple as that, James, but if we don't give it a try how are we to know? Australia is further away and there are plenty who have gone there."

"A lot of them forced to go, for stealing a pig or a cow. My cousin, Francis, for one," said James.

"Well there you are, now. At least myself and Brigid have the option of coming back. Will you not consider it yourself, for your family's sake? We could get some land between us?"

"Ahh, Michael, you are like a dog with a bone but I won't change my mind about going. I am saving to buy my own boat. That is what Mary wants too, and you well know it. Here – hold out your hand to me, Michael."

James dropped something onto his friend's open palm.

"You can't give those away; they were a present from your daughter," protested Michael.

"I want you to have them. Every time you look at these shells, you will be reminded of your roots and that you have a friend there to welcome you back at any time. Go on, Michael, take them. I still have some left in my pocket."

"Even though neither myself nor Brigid can write, I will find someone to put our words into a letter and I promise to keep in touch with you. If ever you change your mind, there will be a place with us over there for you, no matter where we are," Michael was getting choked up with emotion.

"Come on, let's get back inside before we start bawling like a couple of babies,"

146

laughed James, slapping Michael on the back.

Four weeks after Michael and Brigid boarded a ship to New York, James crossed the Irish Sea. Even though the blight hadn't devastated the crop, hardly any potatoes had been planted in 1847 due to the fact that seed potatoes were scarce. Many people had been employed doing public works to earn money for food and rent, so with not enough seeds and labourers, there wasn't much of a harvest to bring in that year. However, it was disease and not starvation that caused most of the deaths of Irish people in the year that came to be known as Black '47.

As the steamship approached the dock, James could see Mary holding Catherine. The excited child was waving with both hands at everyone on board. As he waited patiently to disembark, he inhaled deep into his lungs the salty, seaweed air of home. Even though his stay in England had only been a few months in duration, the time had dragged by for James. He had to remind himself that he wasn't dreaming as he stood watching his family on the quayside. As usual, there were more passengers waiting to get on than off the boat.

When James stepped onto the dockside, Mary rushed into his arms, squashing their daughter between them. Catherine squealed as James kissed her eyes, nose and the top of her head. Mary held onto him, laughing and crying at the same time. Savouring the moment, James would have liked to stand there forever, his wife and child in his arms, enjoying a contentment he had not felt in a long time. A man and his children were standing just behind Mary, looking at the happy reunion, with smiling faces.

"Do I know you?" asked James.

Mary stood back and introduced them.

"This is Thomas Gallagher and his children. They will be boarding the boat you just got off."

"Very happy to meet you, James," Thomas held out his hand. "Your family have been so kind to us, I don't know what we would have done without their help."

"Both you and your son were a great help to Pat in cutting and footing the turf. We were happy to have you stay with us." As she said this, Mary picked up each of the little ones and kissed them before turning her attention to their older brother.

Tom was struggling to remain composed as he removed his cap to shake Mary's hand. Lastly, she shook hands with Thomas, who had been tickling Catherine as she wriggled in her father's arms.

"Have you somewhere to stay when you get over?" asked James, feeling almost like an intruder in the farewells taking place.

"I have a cousin in Liverpool. We will be fine there, until I get on my feet again. I would prefer to live in the countryside if there is work to be got harvesting."

"There's plenty of work for navvies, if you have the stamina for it. Railway tracks are being laid everywhere, you could try that for the winter. You might even earn enough to lease a small farm next year."

"Thank you, James, I will keep that in mind. Well, children, let's go join the queue, it looks like the passengers are starting to board."

Catherine was in her usual spot, high up on a pair of shoulders. James felt as if he had never been away, walking the few miles home from the docks, his wife at his side.

"What was that all about? Why where they staying with you? Are they friends of Pat and Annie's?"

Mary explained how they had come to meet Thomas and his children, leaving out the bit about the knife.

"Oh, James, you should have seen the pitiful state they were in. They walked from Carlow. When Thomas's wife died in the workhouse, he took his children and left. He heard that Dublin was full of fever so instead made for Drogheda, hoping to get a ship to England. There was a fever outbreak there too, so he travelled on up the coast to Dundalk. He had pawned their coats to buy food. When they entered some towns, even though they weren't sick, they were rounded up with other poor unfortunates and put into carts to be driven away and left on the roadside. The fear of strangers carrying the fever drives any bit of compassion out of the hearts of people."

"They were just trying to protect their families and stop the spread of disease," said James. "You saw what it was like in Liverpool, didn't you?"

"I know, I suppose nobody knows how they will act, until they are put in that position. Let's not talk any more of sickness and despair. Tell me about Brigid and Michael's trip to America," Mary changed the subject.

"They invited us over any time we want. Shall we plan a visit there in the spring, my dear?" James spoke in a grand tone of voice.

"Why, Lord McGrother, I do believe we will need a holiday by then – having spent a year without one. Splendid suggestion, if I may be bold enough to say so," mimicked Mary.

They laughed and chased each other until the beach near their home came into view and James ran onto the sand. Pulling seaweed from the rocks, the young man held it to his face, inhaling deeply before draping it over his daughter's head. As they approached the open door to his aunt and uncle's cottage, the wonderful aroma of rabbit stew wafted out.

When Annie had finished smothering him in kisses, Pat grabbed hold of James by the shoulders and looked him up and down.

"Well now, we are still eye to eye. You haven't grown an inch, have you?" his uncle teased.

"I reckon it's you that has shrunk, Uncle Pat."

James sniffed the air and said, "I see you finally outran a poor old rabbit."

The bantering and joking went on all the way through the meal and as Mary looked around the table at her smiling family, she thought of the news she was going to give her husband later that evening. She felt it was a good thing that he was laughing and in great form, as that would probably change when he found out he would have another mouth to feed in the winter.

CHAPTER TWENTY-FIVE

A sound much like a choir of pigs came up through the floor boards. It made James and Mary laugh as they lay side by side, feeling complete once more.

"It sounds like Pat and Annie are speaking to each other in some strange piggy language," whispered Mary, "I don't know how Catherine is staying asleep, down there next to Annie, through all that snoring."

As she leaned away from the mattress to blow out the candle, James turned on his side to face her and propped himself up on an elbow.

"Leave it lit awhile, Mary. I want to keep looking at you."

"James McGrother, you are making me blush. Besides, it's a waste of a candle."

Pulling Mary slowly back onto the mattress, James kept his eyes locked on hers. He ran his fingers lightly down the side of her face, onto her neck and along the length of her arm. Sliding his hand across her abdomen, he let it rest there. Every muscle in Mary's body tensed. James suddenly pulled away from her to sit upright against the wall. He drew his knees towards his chest, without once averting his gaze from her eyes. They stared silently at each other in the soft light. The only movement in the room was the shadow created by the flickering candle flame. The only sound, a symphony of snores from below.

"*He knows, he knows,*" thought Mary.

She had wanted to tell him in the dark, to conceal the anxiety she knew would be written all over her face. Mary closed her eyes and took a deep breath.

"James, I have . . . I am . . ."

"You are carrying our son. I knew it the moment I saw you. Why did you not tell me sooner?"

Mary sat up and hugged him, relieved that he was being so calm about it.

"I thought you might consider it another load to bear, having an extra child to feed. I know times are hard, James, but I feel this is more of a blessing than a burden."

James leaned over his young wife and quenched the candle flame. Lying on his side, he drew Mary into his arms. The moment she was dreading had passed and he had made it easy for her to tell him what she had been avoiding all day.

"What makes you think it's a boy, James?"

He kissed the back of her neck.

"You seem different this time, I don't know what it is, just . . . different. How far along are you? It must have been when you came to see me in England."

"It was, I came back with more than I went over with, didn't I? I certainly feel different this time, I was very sick every morning up till last week. That never happened me on Catherine."

"You were starving on her. The winter that you carried her was a hungry one. At least this time you have some food in your belly to throw up."

James closed his eyes, pretending to drift off to sleep. He thought about returning to England for a few more months before the birth, wanting to make sure Mary was well nourished for her second pregnancy. It was something they could discuss with Pat and Annie. When Mary's breathing changed to a slow rhythm, he knew she had fallen asleep. James kissed her hair and smiled at the thought of her fretting over telling him her news. She really didn't know him as well as she might think.

It was late next morning when the young couple came down the stairs for breakfast. There was some stirabout in the cauldron over the fire, but no sign of Pat, Annie or Catherine. Mary dished up food for James and didn't seem surprised that they were alone in the house.

"Where is everyone? Annie is usually here at this time of the morning, isn't she? Do you think she has taken Catherine for a walk?"

"Oh James, so many questions. Let's just eat and enjoy the peace and quiet before your daughter gets back, shall we?"

"I think I will go find Pat when I have eaten. He's probably mending nets for tonight's fishing. It will be good to get out in the bay after all this time. I missed it almost as much as I missed you, Mary."

"Such a charmer. I'll come with you, the fresh air will do me good."

As they neared the beach, James could see Pat working on the nets while Annie chased Catherine around one of the boats. On their approach, Pat looked up and smiled.

"Ready for a trip out to sea, tonight, son?"

"I am, to be sure, Uncle Pat, and the weather is perfect for it, isn't it?"

Mary caught hold of Catherine and swung her around. She sat the child on her hip while Annie stood beside them. They were all looking at James as he ran his hand over the boat that his uncle's nets were draped upon.

"This is a fine boat, Pat, don't tell me you've joined another crew. Who owns it and can I come out with ye?"

Stepping away from the bow, Pat admitted he had recently decided to sail on another boat and he was sure there would be room for one more crew member. Mary brought Catherine over to the nets that covered the side of the vessel and they lifted them up to reveal what was written on the boat. The name, Mary Catherine, stood out in newly painted, white letters.

"It's yours, James. *Your* crew is the one I joined. There are two other men coming out with us tonight." Pat pointed to the nets and lines that lay across the boat, "And this is your tackle. These are fine nets, James. Thomas Gallagher and his son helped me repair them. He painted the names on the boat, too, being able to read and write, like yourself."

"How can you afford this? Did you borrow the money?" James was still in shock.

Mary grabbed hold of his hand. "We saved every penny you sent over and bought the hens and some seed potatoes. The rest was spent on the boat. Aren't you happy with it, James?" Mary was beginning to think they had made a big mistake.

"Of course I'm happy with it, but I didn't earn nearly enough for a boat like that."

Pat placed a hand on his nephew's shoulder. "Your brothers and sisters made a collection and sent the money over to Mary. Michael contributed, too – in fact it was his idea to get you a boat. When we added it to your savings it was more than enough to buy this one. It came from Annagassan, the man who owned it died and his widow needed the money. Sure what good was it to her? At least now, she can feed her family for a while. All it needed was a bit of work."

James had a lump in his throat and he picked up one of the nets, pretending to inspect it. He was overwhelmed by the generosity shown him.

"Well, if we want to catch any fish tonight we had better make sure our nets are in order, there's no time for all this idle chatter," the young man said, trying to cover his emotions.

Catherine tugged at her father's trouser leg and held out a tiny, closed fist to him. James knelt down on one knee, and placed his hand under hers. As she slowly opened her fingers, three little sea shells dropped onto his palm. James smiled at Mary as he picked up his daughter and kissed her soft curls.

"You will never know how much your wee presents mean to me," he whispered.

THE END

******

Thank you for reading and if you enjoyed this story, there are more in the series. The second book in this saga is called *'A Year of Broken Promises'* and you can find it at this link, along with a video trailer.
https://www.amazon.com/Jean-Reinhardt/e/B00CSMF0VW

REFERENCES

Cover Image

Catherine (Breen) Parker and Seamus
Breen.
The author's mother and brother.

Chapter 7

Navvy, a shorter form of navigator (UK) or
navigational engineer (US), is particularly
applied to describe the manual labourers
working on major civil engineering projects.
The term was coined in the late 18th century
in Great Britain when numerous canals were
being built, which were also sometimes
known as 'navigations', or 'eternal
navigations', intended to last forever.
Many of the navvies employed building the
railways in England in the early part of the
19th century had to live in squalid temporary
accommodations. The navvies working on
the Liverpool and Manchester Railway were
paid daily and their pay reputedly went on
ale and porter, leaving little for food. When
the workers were unfit to work, monies were
deducted from their wages and meal tokens
were issued. These tokens could be handed
in at meal caravans for a bowl of soup and a
portion of bread. At first the token was a slip
of paper called a "flimsy" because of its
thickness. In today's terms it would be

similar to a grade called "bank paper". As these tokens could be copied by the forgers, the Liverpool and Manchester Railway supplied its contractors with six-sided food tokens that were surrendered for meals. These were cut from brass and had the initials LMR stamped upon them. This reduced the problems of drunken navvies and eliminated the local farm labourers freeloading from the food caravans. Tokens and a description of their use can be found in the Museum of Science & Industry in Manchester.

https://en.wikipedia.org/wiki/Navvy

Chapter 14

Drogheda Independent (Newspaper):

THE following notice was posted up along the Steam-packet Quay in Drogheda during the first week in May 1847: *'Notice is Hereby Given'. 'An Order in Council has been issued directing that all Steam-packets arriving in any English port from Ireland shall hoist a yellow flag and remain outside until examined by a medical officer. If any person or persons shall then be found afflicted with fever such person or persons shall be removed to a floating hospital and if sick persons are on a second voyage of the same vessel found on board the vessel must perform quarantine for a number of days according to the state of health of the passengers on board'.*

This harsh notice also stated;
'That no deck passengers can be allowed on board or be taken to Liverpool in any vessel belonging to the Drogheda Steam Packet Company unless examined by some Medical Officer that may be appointed for that service at the port as to their freedom of fever and also that no destitute persons who may not be able to support themselves by their own labour will be allowed to embark between Drogheda Port and Liverpool.
On and after the 12th next (May 1847), the deck fare will be 5 shillings each way'.

As a result of this increase in the fares to England for deck passengers from the port of Drogheda the Drogheda Argus editorial comment made the following observations on this alarming situation;
'We are not at all surprised that the authorities of Liverpool should have become alarmed at the spread of disease in their town within the last few months. The number of emigrants who have landed in Liverpool since the first of January is stated to be 165,000, of these 55,000 have emigrated for America and probably 10,000 were returned to Ireland, leaving 100.000 located in Liverpool or scattered about the country or lying in English graves from the ravages of the pestilence that they brought with them.

Chapter 14

An article in the Manchester Examiner march 1847 a letter from Alexander Somerville:

Seven men were in a field which measured three acres, and such had just been sown with oats. They were employed in breaking the clods of earth, in clearing the furrows for letting off top water, and in otherwise finishing the sowing of the oats. It was about four in the afternoon when I saw them. They appeared to me to work very indifferently; the whole seven were doing less than one man's work. I watched them for some time, while they did not see me, consequently they could not be enacting a part before a stranger. I was soon convinced that the men were, some of them, leaning on their implements of work, and others staggering among the clods, from sheer weakness and hunger. I concluded this to be the case from the frequency of such signs. One of the men, after I had watched them some time, crawled through a gap in the hedge, came out upon the road on his hands and knees, and then tried to rise, and got up bit by bit as a feeble old man might be supposed to do. He succeeded in getting upon his feet at last, and moved slowly away, with tottering steps, towards the village, in a miserable hovel of which was his home.
I thought I would speak to the feeble old man, and followed and came up with him. He was

not an old man. He was under forty years of age; was tall and sinewy, and had all the appearances of what would have been a strong man if there had been flesh on his body. But he bowed down, his cheeks were sunken, and his skin sallow-coloured, as if death were already with him. His eyes glared upon me fearfully; and his skinny skeleton hands clutched the handle of the shovel upon which he supported himself while he stood to speak to me, as it were the last grasp of life.

'It is the hunger, your honour; nothing but the hunger,' he said in a feeble voice: 'I stayed at the work till I could stay no longer. I am fainting now with the hunger. I must go home and lie down. There is six children and my wife and myself. We had nothing all yesterday, (which was Sunday,) and this morning we had only a handful of yellow meal among us all, made into a stirabout, before I came out to work–nothing more and nothing since. Sure this hunger will be the death of all of us. God have mercy upon me and my poor family.'

I saw the poor man and his poor family, and truly might he say, 'God have mercy!' They were skeletons all of them, with skin on the bones and life within the skin. A mother skeleton and baby skeleton; a tall boy skeleton, who had no work to do; who could do nothing but eat, and had nothing to eat. Four female children skeletons, and the tall father skeleton, not able to work to get food

162

for them, and not able to get enough of food when he did work for them. Their only food was what his wages of 10 d. per day would procure of 'yellow meal' – the meal of the Indian corn. The price of that was 3s. per stone of 16 lb. This gave for the eight persons 26 lb. 10 oz. of meal for seven days; being about seven ounces and a half per day for each person. No self-control could make such persons distribute such a starvation of food over seven days equally. Their natural cravings made them eat it up at once, or in one, or three days at most, leaving the other days blank, making the pangs of hunger still worse.

But in the calculation I am supposing all the wages go for meal. I believe none of it was expended on anything else, not even salt, save fuel: fuel in this village must all be purchased by such people; they are not allowed to go to the bogs to cut it for themselves. Nor is this the season to go to the bogs, if they were allowed. The fuel required to keep the household fire merely burning, hardly sufficient to give warmth to eight persons around it, to say nothing of half-naked persons, would cost at least sixpence a day. Wherefore, no fuel was used by this family, nor by other working families, but what was required to boil the meal into a stirabout

The following books proved to be a great source of information in the writing of this story. They are full of well documented events and photographs of people whose families have lived in Blackrock for many generations:

The Parish of Haggardstown & Blackrock – A History by Noel Sharkey.
First Printed in 2003 by Dundalgan Press (W. Tempest) Ltd., Dundalk.
The Parish of Haggardstown & Blackrock – A Pictorial Record
Compiled and written by Noel Sharkey with photos by Owen Byrne.
Printed in 2008 by Dundalgan Press (W. Tempest) Ltd., Dundalk.

30711339R00099

Printed in Great
Britain
by Amazon